INDIGO TEXTILES

First published in the United Kingdom 1989
by A & C Black (Publishers) Limited
35 Bedford Row, London WC1R 4JH

ISBN 0–7136–3129–5

A CIP catalogue record for this book is available from the British Library.

First published in the USA 1989 by Lark Books
50 College Street, Asheville, NC 28801

ISBN 0–937274–40–2

LC Catalog Card Number: 88–45225

Filmset by August Filmsetting, Haydock, St Helens
Printed in the DDR by Interdruck, Leipzig

Every effort has been made to ensure that all
information in this book is accurate. However,
owing to differing conditions, tools, dyestuffs and
individual skills, the publisher cannot be
responsible for any injuries, losses or other damage
which may result from the use of the information in
this book.

For imperial measurements, use measuring cups
with fluid ounces marked or standard American
measuring spoons (flat, not heaped, spoonfuls).

Chinese character for indigo
The character for indigo occurs in China's oldest
literary source book, *Shi jing* (*The Singers' book*)
which was compiled in the first half of the first
millennium BC.

The character for the word lan (early Chinese
glam) consists of a radical or meaning-giver sig-
nifying *plant* or *grass*. The lower part of the character serves as a phoneticum, indicating its
sound. When used independently this sign has
two interpretations: jian (even accent) means
'to regard'; jian with a falling accent means 'to
mirror yourself'. This character, which was
originally read as klam, is composed of three
graphic elements: eye, person and vessel: a person who mirrors himself in a vessel with water in
it.

Göran Malmqvist, Professor of Sinology,
Stockholm University

INDIGO TEXTILES

Technique and History

Gösta Sandberg

A & C Black • London
Lark Books • Asheville North Carolina

It is not long since Indian blue, or indigo (Indicum) was first imported. It costs 7 denarii a pound.

Pliny (1st century AD)

Large quantities of indigo of excellent quality are manufactured here. It is prepared from a plant which is pulled up by the root and placed in a barrel of water, where it lies until the plants have rotted; then the juices are pressed out. When this juice has been exposed to the sun and has evaporated, a sort of dough remains, which is cut into small pieces of the size and shape we see.

Marco Polo (end of 13th century)

There is much dispute as to what sort of plant Nil or Anil (Indigo) is.

Johan Linder (1720)

Flowering indigo grown by Dorothy Miller of California, USA.

ACKNOWLEDGEMENTS

The material for this book has been collected and written over a number of years. Journeys to distant places and contacts with fabric-printers, blue-dyers and dyeing-technologists in different parts of the world have all deepened my knowledge of indigo.

A number of traveller-friends, ethnographers and textile-scientists have kindly placed their own material at my disposition. Of these I must mention the 'Africa Group' of Karin Wallin, Eva Lutteman, Lena Nordström and Lena Nygårds, and the 'Japan Group' of Margareta Bergstrand, Lova Lindroos, Eva Lagnert and Kazuko Tamura.

It has been a special pleasure to be able to have the cooperation in the shaping of this book of my close friends, former pupils and a couple of my own children.

As the number of collaborators, due to the size of the subject, has been large and the size of the book limited, my thanks to them must be brief and rather summary. But may they all know that I am profoundly grateful for their help, often over many years, in producing 'the blue book'.

Some, who perhaps have helped more than others here, are due my specially warm thanks. Above all, my friend Jan Sisefsky, who undertook much difficult translation and interpreted the Chinese calligraphy, as well as reading the MS with a critical eye. Then Märta Lindström who read and commented on the first historical section of the book. Then Nils Lindström of Svenska ICI and P.O. Larson of Diazo-Kemi AB who similarly checked the latter part of the book dealing with the technicalities of dyeing. I have had valuable advice, too, from Kerstin Gustafsson, Lena Ringensson and Inger Öhrn. Much work of translation has been done for me by Olle and Elisabeth Sandberg during several years. The calligraphy of the Chinese character for indigo was drawn by Dr T'ien Lung. Professor Göran Malmqvist has provided the analysis of the character. Their help has been a special inspiration for this book.

I am especially indebted to Lena Nessle for her help in shaping the book with illustrations, photographs etc.

Last, but by no means least, I must thank my wife, Gunnel, whose kindness and generosity helped me so much in my work, as well as for her advice and encouragement.

CONTENTS

A PORTRAIT OF THE AUTHOR

The author in word and photograph

Gösta Sandberg, expert, teacher and author of books on textiles, dyes and manufacturing techniques, lives in Nora, a very Swedish little town with a church and a square on the shore of a lake. In this typically Swedish countryside he has assembled a huge international collection of textiles and information about textiles. The emphasis is on popular country textiles, so often overlooked and ignored by the art historian. Emphasis lies, too, on the craftsmanship and traditional knowledge which today risk being lost. The third point of emphasis is on the colour – indigo. Here you will find a small worn, but lovingly patched, indigo-coloured piece of ikat from Japan, pieces of cloth from West Africa, batik collected during Gösta's travels in Indonesia, Macedonian embroideries from his travels there, plangi from China and the same knotting-technique in an ornamental scarf from Jämtland in Sweden. There are about two thousand items in the collection, all carefully documented and preserved.

It all provides present delight and food for future thought. Technique advances, we say, yet never again will linen be woven with over 330 weft threads per inch (130 per centimetre) as was being done in Egypt thousands of years before our era began. Never again will cotton cloth be woven so thin as that of the bare-footed weavers of Madapalam and Calcutta, who made it all by hand in what we now call undeveloped India. Never again, despite machines and technique, can a thread be spun so fine that one kilometre of it weighs scarcely more than a gramme, as they once did with little distaffs. We say that machines and mechanisation give people more time. Yet never again will anyone have the time, and be able to afford to devote two years to weaving, say, a double ikat in Gujarat or a batik for a bridal cloak in Java. The collection queries many of our ideas of what knowledge is and time means, and makes your mind reel.

The motive power behind Gösta's collecting and search for knowledge has been respect for craftsmanship and skill as is found, for example, in batik from Java, and in blueprint from Japan. 'An expertise and a culture that we more primitive Westerners can neither imitate nor fully understand' as Gösta once put it. He likes to point to the skill and cultural role of women in Indonesia; all heavier and less skilled work is done by men, while the more demanding batik work is the women's domain. Pradnjaparmita, the Hindu goddess, is the highest expression of wisdom and womanliness. 'And there is something in that,' he says, alluding to our male-dominated society with its motor cars and atomic weapons.

I first visited Gösta Sandberg in 1978. Then, as now, his indigo kimono, white Chinese embroidery for *ai* and *zome* – indigo and dye – hangs in the lobby. A Chinese calligrapher once dubbed him – *Saiv ge shi*, the man who spreads systematic knowledge, and he certainly deserves the name. As late as 1959 quite incorrect recipes for dyeing with indigo and sulphuric acid were still being published. Today's correct hot-bath method is one of the skills this learned man has disseminated. And now here comes a whole book.

Karin Wallin

9

AUTHOR'S FOREWORD

Indigo, the blue dye, was known and used several thousand years before the start of the Christian era. Of all natural dye-stuffs indigo is not only justly the oldest, but the most important. Various patterning techniques for textiles in various parts of the world are intimately linked with it. This is especially true of a number of West African, Asian and Central European resist techniques, which were long largely unknown to us. It is only in recent years that a number of exhibitions have provided opportunities for getting to know the rare and so very different treasures of 'foreign' cultures. However, before we can understand them and put their unique value to meaningful use, we have to familiarise ourselves with the dyes on which these textiles entirely depend. One difficulty encountered here has been the lack of any comprehensive or profound study of the dye-stuff and its use.

The intention behind this book has been to provide a picture of 'the living colour', its history, techniques and aesthetic value, without straying into petty detail of dye-technology. I have, too, considered it important to describe some of the resist techniques directly linked to the possibilities of dyeing with indigo, which are important and treasured in the cultures where they are used. They tell of distant epochs and lands and peoples beyond our narrow circle. The day when we can no longer appreciate the vitality of an African *lappa*, the grace of a Javanese *selendang* or the sophisticated forms of a Japanese *haori*, we shall have lost something of prime importance.

Indigo's history is longer and its significance greater than those of any other dye-stuff. There is more to write about on indigo than of any other dye, so much so that it is impossible to include it all in one book. I have, therefore, preferred to describe individual events, conditions and people, which like the bright points in a galaxy of stars, will allow the observer to see the picture as he interprets it and what it means to him.

Gösta Sandberg
Nora, May, 1986

The Queen Kén Dedés, incarnation of the highest exponent of wisdom and womanliness, the goddess Pradnjaparamita. A stone sculpture of the 13th century in Singasari in eastern Java. The figure's dress reproduces the djilamprang motif, which is so familiar from the pattern-flora of batik.

And Mordecai went out from the presence of the king in royal apparel of blue and white, and with a great crown of gold, and with a garment of fine linen and purple, and the city of Shushan rejoiced and was glad.

Esther, 8

INTRODUCTION

On the colour of kings and the king of colours

Down through the ages two colours have influenced mankind more than any others: deep-blue *indigo* and red *purple*. In many respects they are opposites, yet on occasion they can complement each other and work together. One is obtained from the vegetable, the other from the animal kingdom. As colours, the first is what we are accustomed to call a *cold* colour, though with a hint of warmth, the other a *warm* colour with a touch of coldness. This affinity may well appear fortuitous, but in reality it is more than that.

That these two colours acquired a special position among textile dye-stuffs was not due to their chromatic merits, but rather to other, more weighty factors. Writing on the subject, the French statesman Colbert stated: 'It is not enough for a dye to be lovely, it must also be good and last as long as the material it adorns.' Though this statement was made relatively recently, it expresses a central, important requirement

of textile manufacture, a requirement that in remoter times, and in certain circumstances, would decide whether a dye was used or not. In other words, the dye with the best imaginable practical qualities – what we today call fastness – was valued, given status and became reserved for those who themselves enjoyed high estate. That dyes could be chosen for aesthetic reasons is a relatively modern phenomenon.

Archaeological finds in Egypt, China and the Indus Valley show that textile skills were highly developed even several thousand years before the Christian era began. It is not so easy to determine when and where the dyeing of textiles began. For the time being we must content ourselves with determining by modern methods the age of individual finds and what dye was employed. Analysis has shown that several different dyes were used for textiles in Egypt as early as the second millennium BC. The same is true of Chinese grave goods which reveal a high standard of dyeing technique even in prehistoric times. However, most of the material of the Egyptian grave finds is undyed; coloured garments are rarities. What the people of the Nile valley wore were almost exclusively garments of undyed linen; and even the Greeks, for whom flax was an important agricultural product,

Map of India from Th. Salmon's *Hedendaagsche Historie of Tegenwoordige Staat van Alle Volkeren*, published in Amsterdam in 1731. On it lie purple shells and pieces of indigo.

never dyed it. It was the same in many other parts of the world.

In all ages, each community, whether large or small, has been governed by a ruling class, membership of which was indicated by some clear distinguishing mark or badge of status. Dress provided an early means of doing this. A ruler would decide not only how he himself was to be clad, but also how his subjects were *not* to dress and what colours they were *not* to wear. That is why the study of the occurrence and importance of colour in antiquity is in many respects a study of the ruling classes' choice of colours. Grave goods can tell us how the kings and princes dressed, but not what the weavers and dyers wore.

When clothes, or parts of apparel, were to be dyed, two things were required of the dye to be used: it had to be able to be absorbed by the material in question; and secondly, it had to be absolutely fast. In many a civilisation blue from an indigo-producing plant was the only dye that met these requirements.

The technical superiority of indigo rests on the fact that it is what dyers call a *substantive* dye or fermentation-bath dye, indeed, the only one the vegetable kingdom has to offer. It will dye both vegetable and animal fibres and does so with results that cannot be achieved even approximately using any other vegetable dye.

If we go far back in time and space we find the colour blue associated with power, magic and divinity. The Egyptians even reserved the use of blue for royalty and we are told that the daughters of the pharaoh painted their breasts blue and gold. During the excavations at Thebes an indigo-coloured garment was among the things found. This is assumed to be from the days of the Old Kingdom (2500 BC), or possibly older. Linen threads in one princess's dress (of 1000 BC) are considered likely to have been dyed with woad. In India, the true colour of the sun as god of life and procreation was blue. Krishna, the best loved divinity of Hinduism and the god of love, is usually depicted blue and surrounded by lovelies whose palms and the soles of whose feet are henna coloured. The nobility of ancient Guatemala denoted their position by wearing blue, and the mighty Odin, of the Nordic sagas, always dressed in blue. It is not easy to chart the origin of Asiatic indigo and its path westwards. An unfortunately anonymous traveller of AD 60–80, who compiled various treatises on navigation and geography, tells us that fine cloth materials, spices, jewels and indigo were at that period sent from India to Egypt. Pliny, who calls it indico, informs us that it enjoyed a great reputation, since it came from India. Up to the 12th century people had the strangest idea about it. They took it to be a mineral which you mined like ore and so they called it 'Indian stone'. It was Marco Polo who first corrected this peculiar idea of indigo's origin, preparation and use.

Indigo has always been of considerable local importance, but it didn't become of universal significance until it was cultivated systematically and on a large scale to feed the new trade outlets opened up in the 17th and 18th centuries. For a couple of hundred years the dark-blue dye, indigo, dominated world trade, ruined princely houses and taught the West that there was yet another world beyond the seas and the Caucasus.

Naturally enough indigo acquired a variety of local names. The traditional Indian word for blue was *nil*, the same as was used for the dye, and then the Arabs and Egyptians took the name over and changed it slightly to *anil*. Linnaeus named the plant family *Indigofera*, after its land of origin and the Latin verb *fero*, to produce.

The indigo plant does not produce the actual dye-stuff ready made, so to speak, but in the form of a colourless, crystallising substance called indican. When the parts of the plant are subjected to fermentation, an enzyme which is present particularly in the leaves, produces indigo. This is insoluble in water, but an alkaline reduction can turn it into a solution in which dyeing can be achieved. When the textile-material is lifted from the dye-bath, the dye-stuff is transformed by the action of the oxygen in the air back into its original insoluble state, only by now it has been absorbed into the dyed fibres.

A question often asked, though always difficult to answer, is how people in the first place ever hit on the complicated procedure involved in obtaining and using indigo. One suggestion is that someone once noticed how a heap of damp indigo leaves, that had lain undisturbed for a long time, had spontaneously formed a bluish mass which stained your hands and whatever came in contact with it, at first inadvertently and then deliberately. In all probability the earliest dye-baths were what we today call fermentation-baths in which the indigo's dye-stuff is dissolved with the help of micro-organisms and an alkaline substance like lime or lye. This primitive method scarcely changed at all, and is still employed in many parts of Africa and East Asia.

In the ancient civilisations around the Mediterranean indigo was for a long while subject to penal taxation, especially before other dyes, especially red, began to be used. A belt found in Tutankhamun's grave (he died in 1550 BC) has been shown to have been dyed with alizarin, the dye-stuff of madder. However, its fastness was not good either in this or in the other finds, which shows that the technique of binding dye-stuff to fibres with mordant metallic salts had not then been discovered.

Purple

Gradually it became possible to produce a red colour which had qualities just as good as those of indigo. This was *purple* and for a long time it vied with indigo for pre-eminence as a colour for the highest in society. In the history of dyeing the story of purple is as imaginatively stimulating as it is mysterious.

We know that purple-dyeing was done very early in South America and along the coasts of the Indian Ocean, but of when and how it came to be used by the Mediterranean civilisations we know very little. The remains of cloth found in graves there have been so few and insignificant that there is scarcely enough to be analysed. No actual recipe has survived, so all we have is Pliny's incomplete account of dyeing with purple. The literary evidence is more extensive, for no ancient writer omitted to mention the precious purple dye which is mentioned in so many places in the Bible. It is recorded in *Exodus* that 'a hanging for the tabernacle was made of blue and purple and scarlet, and fine twined linen, wrought with needlework'.

The purple dye is obtained from a mollusc, one of the *Muricidae*, especially from those members of the family that live in the Mediterranean, murex and nucella. The molluscs were collected by fishermen who dived down to the banks where they grew on the bottom, choosing the oldest and largest specimens which were hoisted up to the surface in wicker baskets. The mantle inside the mollusc's quite insignificant shell is the purple gland, which secretes a greyish-yellow substance which contains the precious dye-stuff in its preliminary stage. This gland they cut out and salted. Several days later a brownish fluid had formed and this was diluted with water and urine and the whole boiled up in leaden vessels for about ten days. The evaporated remains were mixed with honey and urine (this was probably the beginning of fermentation) after which the skeins of yarn could be dipped into the bath.

The main centres of production of purple were the Phoenician cities of Tyre and Sidon (the present day Salda) in Lebanon, where long stretches of the beach are still covered with a layer of crushed murex shells several feet deep bearing witness to the activity that once brought the two cities enormous wealth. Gradually, however, due to excessive harvesting and slow regeneration of the mollusc, their numbers declined. It was not long after this that the Greeks, who had long sought to discover the secret of the purple, came across banks of the precious molluscs along their own coasts. Reduced supplies of the molluscs combined with the introduction of cheap imitations made from *Alcanna tinctoria* and *Orsellic* shook the foundations of the old purple dynasty; then, when the Turks conquered Constantinople in 1453 and destroyed the Byzantine empire, the entire production of purple was lost along with much else, including the knowledge that had been accumulated through the centuries of its production and methods of dyeing.

At the beginning of this century a German chemist, Paul Friedländer, thought that he had discovered how to produce the Tyrian purple of the ancients synthetically. To make certain about this he decided to investigate the old dye, an investigation that produced a number of unexpected results. The first of these was the enormous quantity of molluscs required to produce a given quantity of the dye-stuff. Twelve thousand molluscs produced only a minute amount of the pure dye-stuff. Next, was the sensational discovery that chemically the purple was identical with the dye-stuff obtained from indigo, apart from two atoms of bromine it has where indigo has hydrogen. Friedländer considered that this proved that the purple, like indigo, was a fermentation-bath, substantive dye. Later research by others has shown that all mollusc purple has indigo-blue in it, though in varying quantities. Careless fermenting can turn the purple dye-stuff into indigo.

There are two varieties of purple molluscs in the Mediterranean: *Murex brandaris* which produces the 'red purple' (the *purpura blatta* of antiquity), a kind of beetle, and *Murex trunchulus* which produces the 'blue purple' (*purpura hyacinthina*). The Roman writer Vitruvius distinguishes clearly in his writings between red and blue purples. Sixteen different kinds of things dyed purple are listed in a decree of the Emperor Diocletian.

We have seen how in the course of history the two colours switched roles; indigo, from having been the colour of pharaohs, princes and deities, the few and the select, becoming a colour for the many and for the jackets worn by Chinese peasants, the wrappers of the African women who cultivated cassava and the cloths of the blue-printers of Burgenland. It was a colour whose unsurpassed qualities earned it the title of 'king of colours'. Purple which sometimes in antiquity took over the rôle of the colour for society's dignitaries, the colour for emperors, popes and cardinals, came to be called 'the colour of kings' instead. But despite its title and the importance it enjoyed during a limited period, it was to remain a mere interlude in the history of dyeing. Today it exists only as a name.

'Dyes may come and dyes may go but indigo goes on for ever.'

Organic News

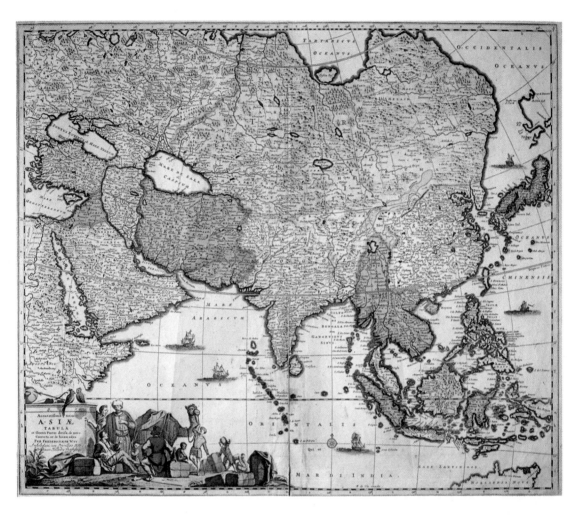

Coloured map of Asia printed in Amsterdam about 1700. In the Middle Ages and long before then camel caravans had brought textiles, jewels and spices along the Silk Road from China to the Far East and the Mediterranean area. From the 16th century on such goods were conveyed by sea instead. Portuguese, Dutch and British ships dominated this trade in cloth and dye-stuffs from India, and spices, rice and coffee from Indonesia.

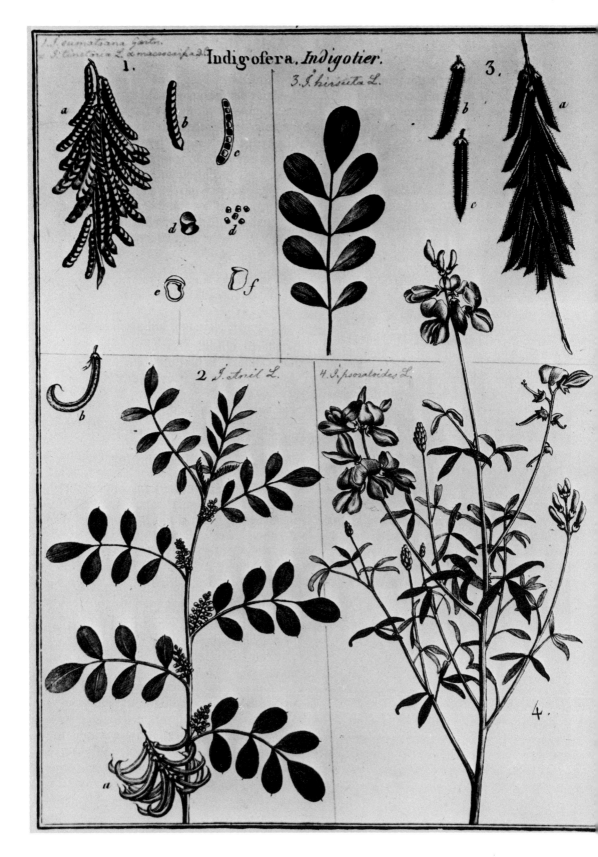

Indigofera. *Indigotier*.

'The noble man says: "Blue comes from the indigo plant, but is more blue than the plant itself . . ."'
from the introduction to an essay by Xun Zi (about 312 BC)

THE INDIGO PLANT

The Dye-stuff and its Extraction

The deep blue indigo colour of textiles, wherever in the world they have been made, always has the same suggestive, almost sombre resonance. However worn and faded, the material yet retains its strange lustre. To us the colour seems the strongest imaginable contrast to the light, graceful form of the plant itself and its red flowers that are like butterflies.

Of the many plants that can produce indigo *one* came to acquire greater significance than the others, that which we know as *Indigofera tinctoria*, so named and described by Linnaeus in his *Species Plantarum* of 1753. Like the other kinds of *indigofera*, *I. tinctoria* belongs to that genus of leguminous plants that are sometimes, much more

Engraving from Lamarck's *Recueil de Planches Botaniques* for the *Encyclopédie* of 1779.

Natural indigo is obtained from a number of plants, each different, but above all from species belonging to the Indigofera family. Among the best are *I. tinctoria*, native to India and China; *I. anil* from South and Central America; *I. sumatrana* and *Baptisia tinctoria* originally from the East Indies, but latterly also cultivated in most parts of the tropics; and Gara, *Lonchocarpus cyanescens*, which is widely used in West Africa. *Polygonum tinctoria* has been the indigo-producing plant most used in Japan.

poetically, called 'butterfly flowers'. They are shrubs that grow to a height of between four and five feet ($1-1\frac{1}{2}$ m), and were originally native in India, China, Indonesia and the northern parts of South America.

In India, the indigo bush used to grow wild almost everywhere. In certain regions where conditions were especially favourable to it, a larger yield of higher quality was obtained, and it was in these areas that the first actual production of indigo began. For the cultivated indigo plant to give a good yield of high, even quality, great care was necessary in all stages of its cultivation, not least important being the preparation of the soil itself with repeated ploughing, harrowing and rolling. The last procedure just before sowing was performed by women and children, who, with stout sticks, broke up any remaining lumps of earth and also cleared the ground of weeds and waste from the previous season's growth.

Indigo seeds – sometimes ready sprouted – were sown at the end of March or the beginning of April. They germinated after four or five days and in the middle of June, which was when the actual production of indigo really began, the plants would have reached the height of a man, if conditions had been favourable. Too much or too little rain could hazard the entire harvest. Normally, a further one or two crops could be obtained at intervals of a couple of months.

19

The harvesting of the indigo bushes usually began in the middle of June just before they flowered. This was men's work for which they used special knives to cut down the plants. Here it was important that each plant should be cut in exactly the right place, neither too high, nor too low down, but just two hands' breadth above the ground. If the cuts were made too high up the yield would be diminished; while too low a cut could injure the young shoots that came up from the root and would yield a fresh harvest in two or three months' time.

The plants were grown in large open fields, where in the middle of the day the heat was what we would consider intolerable, sometimes above 100°F (40°C) in the shade; but the plants were cut in the early morning before the worst of the heat, bundled up and quickly taken to the factory, where large rectangular fermentation vats awaited them. The plants were placed upright in the vat to make it easy for the air in the bundles to escape, and also to enable the fluid to run off quickly after completion of the preliminary process. A vat of some 1,000 cubic feet could hold between 1100 and 1500 pounds (500–700 kg) of indigo plants which were covered with a number of bamboo poles weighted down with a couple of massive baulks of wood before the liquid was allowed in, that is to say water from a reservoir at a higher level. The vat was filled with the water until it was within an inch or two of the wooden baulks. For the next few hours nothing special happened, for it took quite a long time for the indigo leaves to become saturated. But as soon as this had been achieved, the desired process of fermentation began by itself. Sure indications of this happening were a rise in the level of the water in the vat and the formation on leaves and stalks of fine bubbles that gradually detached themselves and rose to the surface in an ever-thickening stream. Before long, the entire vat was seething and bubbling and eventually the surface was covered with a thick layer of scum. Towards the end of the process, which took a day and

a half to complete, repeated tests were made to determine how far the process of fermentation had progressed. This was determined partly by the smell, but mostly by the taste of the fluid. An hour too long of fermentation could endanger the entire yield of months of labour.

As soon as blue scum appeared on the surface, the smell and taste of the liquid was again tested, for now it was merely a matter of minutes. As soon as the liquid tasted sweet and was dark blue in colour, it was quickly drawn off from the vat into a tank on a lower level, where women and girls stood ready with long bamboo sticks in their hands. As soon as the tank was full they began stirring and beating the liquid. With rhythmic movements of the whole body they whipped the liquid until the entire surface was covered with a thick layer of scum which started by being blue, but became whiter and whiter towards the end and then disappeared altogether.

After close on a couple of hours of this whisking, the liquid became more and more yellow-brown and patches of dark blue began to appear. It was then left alone so that the blue patches, which were composed of the dye-stuff now being formed, might settle on the bottom. To hasten the process, soda, lye, powdered unslaked lime, sugar-of-lead, a decoction of parts of plants containing tanning agents and other such things might be added.

As, towards the end of the 19th century, the scale of cultivation of indigo became even larger, the methods of extraction were rationalised. Instead of oxygen being supplied to the bath by whipping the liquid with sticks, this was now done by blowing in air through perforated tubes lowered into the bath. Sometimes, large wheels fitted with paddles or chains that whipped the liquid were used instead.

The first process to which the vegetable mass was subjected, that of fermentation, induced an enzyme reaction that released the indigo proper from its primary state of indican; when oxygen was added during the

subsequent 'whipping', this was oxidised and so turned into indigo blue, indogotin, what in everyday parlance we now call indigo. But a further couple of processes remained, before the circle of production was complete.

It took a couple of hours after the 'whipping' stopped for all the patches of blue to have settled onto the bottom of the bath. That achieved, the liquid was drawn off, leaving all the indigo in a corner of the bottom of the slightly tilted vat. This was then filtered and fed into an iron container for 'boiling', though in practice this entailed only heating it to between 176–212°F (80–100°C). The object of heating the indigo in this way was to eliminate impurities and to stop the enzyme reaction. Boiling was followed by a final process of draining off and filtering through specially stout linen cloth in which the indigo collected in the form of a more or less thick layer of

Production of indigo, from Diderot's *Encyclopédie* of 1753. This involves fermentation of parts of the plant in tanks filled with water, removal of irrelevant particles, threshing of the liquid with sticks of bunches of twigs, purification of the mass obtained and pressing this into balls or cakes.

21

paste, which was then pressed into 22 lb (10 kilo) lumps, later to be cut into handier cubes of 4 oz (100–120 g) on each of which the factory's stamp was impressed.

The final stage of this long, complicated process was for the cubes of indigo to be dried for two or three months in a special shed where the cubes were protected from direct sunlight. If the drying process was too quick the cubes would split or crack, thereby fetching a lower price on the indigo market.

There has never been a recognised universal procedure for producing indigo. Ways and means have altered in different places and under different technical management. The principles, however, have been the same whether the indigo was being produced under European management in West India or by native growers in Bengal.

Although the indigo plant grew wild in most parts of India, the English buyers early confined their attention to that produced in Gujarat. It was in western India, too, that they first organised their own plantations and factories. They would appear to have chosen the right location, for this was the area described by Marco Polo in the 13th century as producing 'ginger, pepper and indigo in abundance'.

The indigo was transported to Europe in specially constructed, iron-bound chests known as 'indigo-chests'. These were often made of fragrant cedar-wood, reddish-brown in colour and with a faint, but pleasant smell, and they were eagerly bought by cabinet-makers and violin-makers. Sometimes the indigo was packed in untanned skins, sewn together and bound with stout ropes.

There were several different qualities of indigo, each with its special name:

Bengal indigo This came from different districts in Bengal and was considered the best. It could be very good, average and ordinary, as far as quality went, and blue, violet and purple in colour, plus various other shades.

Java indigo This was the Indonesian sort, which was usually equally good, but in certain places was preferred for dyeing cotton (cold bath). It was produced mostly in the form of round cakes or pear-shaped pieces. By the end of the 19th century the annual production had exceeded a million pounds (half a million kilos), all sold through Amsterdam and Rotterdam.

Chinese indigo The best qualities of this could compete with the Bengal product. It was mostly sold as thin sheets, $\frac{3}{8}''$ (1 cm) thick, packed in rectangular wooden chests lined with lead-foil and weighing about 88 lb (40 kilos).

Guatemala indigo was of excellent quality, fully comparable with the Indian. It was sold in leather packages containing some 165 lb (75 kilos) of irregular chunks of different sizes.

Manilla indigo was mostly of ordinary quality and contained a lot of earth and lime. Most of what was produced went to America and it was never common on the European market.

African (Senegal) and *Egyptian indigo* varied in quality. Some was very good and could on occasion appear on the market. Production, however, was relatively modest and never of real significance.

Indigo was always expensive and most sought after, even when production was at its height at the end of the 19th century. Its value meant that it was the subject of more or less successful attempts at falsification which buyers had to guard against. The big trading houses and dye-works could test a new parcel of indigo in their own laboratories when it was offered to them, while smaller concerns had to rely on test dyeing.

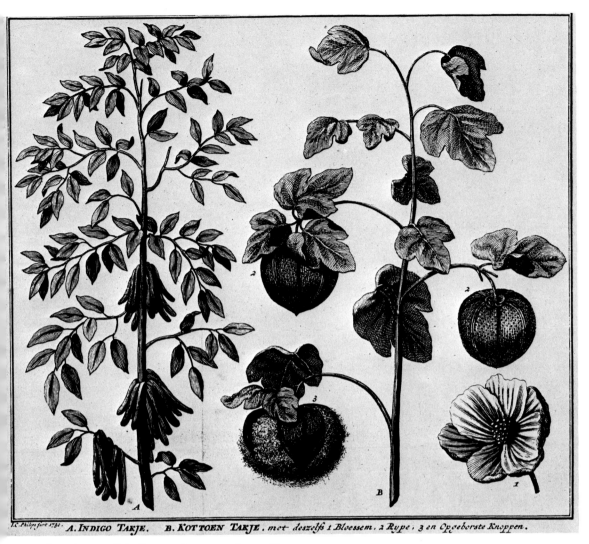

J.C.Philps fecit 1730. A. INDIGO TAKJE. B. KOTTOEN TAKJE. met deszelfs 1 Bloessem, 2 Rype, 3 en Opgeborste Knoppen.

The plants of indigo and cotton from Th. Salmon's book of 1731.

'Cotton is obtained in large quantities from a tree measuring some six fathoms in height and which yields produce for twenty years. However, the cotton from so old a tree is not spun, but used as stuffing. That obtained from trees twelve years old is well suited for muslins and other cloths of the finest make.'

Marco Polo on Malabar on the west coast of India.

'The Britons all dye themselves with woad to make them look terrifying in battle.'

Pliny

WOAD

The Contest between Woad and Indigo

Indigo, the principal dye of Asiatic civilisations, was used for thousands of years prior to the Christian era, yet remained to all intents and purposes unknown in Europe until the Middle Ages. Mention was made of it by Vitruvius, Dioscorides and Caesar, and, centuries later, Marco Polo told his sceptical contemporaries of this remarkable dye that was found in such quantities in India. He explained that it was prepared and used with textiles and even showed them samples that he had brought back to Venice with him. But the little that made its way to Europe along the Silk Road, or via the Red Sea, was insignificant as far as contemporary dyeing went and was used almost solely in the manufacture of ink or as an expensive painter's pigment.

However, since the earliest times a blue dye has been used in Europe. This was a native product prepared from the leaves of the woad plant, which indeed, in chemical composition, methods of use and colour, was the same as indigo. Linnaeus gave it the name of *Isatis tinctoria*, isatis from the Greek 'sazo', meaning 'I smooth', because of the plant's properties of removing swellings and smoothing the skin. (*Tinctoria* means dyeing.) The woad plant is easily recognised thanks to its blue-green colour, sturdy rosettes of leaves and profuse bunched heads of small yellow flowers. It is widespread, growing from Central Europe and the Mediterranean countries, across Russia, Western and Central Asia to China and Japan.

The many finds made during archaeological excavations in the North bear witness to the fact that woad was used there in prehistoric times. Bronze Age garments dyed blue and brown have been found in Denmark, while seeds and pieces of the plant were discovered in Norway's Oseberg ship of the Viking Age.

Nor was woad unknown to the inhabitants of the British Isles, as the quotation from Pliny at the start of this chapter shows. Elsewhere he describes the Roman legions' unusual encounter with blue-dyed Celts in AD 44 and 45: 'Omnes vero se Britanni vitro inficiunt, quod caeruleum efficit colorem, atque horribiliores sunt in pugna aspectu.' ('All Britons dye themselves with woad which makes them blue, in order that in battle their appearance be more terrible.')

The woad plant, a hand-coloured woodcut from L. Fuch's *Flora*, 1545.

Long before Asiatic indigo was introduced into Europe, people there used a native blue dyestuff prepared from the leaves of the woad plant.

Isatis satiua.
Beymisch Weydt.

Ioáus

Glasto.

Guado.

Ad Scorbuti Curationem Utile, ad hir

Tests made in BASF's laboratories some years ago provided even older evidence that the Celts had mastered the art of dyeing with woad. The tests were made on some textile fragments found in the grave of a Celtic prince of the 5th century BC in Altrier (Luxembourg) and these proved them to have been dyed with woad. During the analysis of the extracted dye it was possible to see the characteristic green which distinguishes dyeing with woad from dyeing with indigo. The dye-stuff obtained from woad contains, as well as indigo blue, quantities of a flavin dye-stuff which produces a yellow colour. These two form the tell-tale green of woad.

We can assume that the production of the dye-stuff and the process of dyeing in olden days were the same as those employed with other indigo-producing plants. But there is little or no literary evidence of this. Only one collection of the recipes of antiquity has survived. This is Egyptian and was found in 1828 during excavations near Thebes. A few years later it found its way to Sweden and since then has been known as the *Papyrus Holmiensis*. Its author and its age are both uncertain, but it is assumed to have been written in the first two or three centuries AD. The directions it gives seem to indicate that the recipe itself can be considerably older. The first, concerned with the manufacture and use of woad, is given here, somewhat abbreviated.

This was obviously a true urine-bath and fairly uncomplicated. The use of soapwort (*Saponaria officinalis*) is interesting. One can imagine it acting as an equalising agent and helping to dye the wool through and through. Another interesting passage is the final treating with Orsellic (*Rocella* sp.) which evidently was intended to give a more reddish hue to the dark-blue.

Swedish dyers continued to use woad until well into the 19th century, as often as not in combination with indigo, but had ceased to do so altogether by the end of the century. What one can read about its cultivation and production was written at a time when woad was of significance in the economy. The following details are taken, much abbreviated, from what Professor Adrian Gadd wrote in Åbo in 1750:

To dye dark blue. (From the *Papyrus Holmiensis*)

Cut down the woad and place it all together in a basket in the shade. Break the stems into pieces and let them lie a whole day. On the following day let the air in by trampling them, so that the pieces are thrown up by your feet as they move, and dry thoroughly. Put it in baskets and put them in store. Woad treated in this way is known as 'kol'.

Take about 1 talent (*c.*55 lb or 25 kilos) of woad and place it in the sun in a tank with a capacity of at least 15 *metren* (*c.*150 gallons or 600 litres) and pack it tightly. Then pour urine in until it covers the woad and let this heat in the sun. Next day trample round in the woad in the sun so that all is well soaked. This must be done during three days.

Divide the woad and the urine in which it is soaking into three parts. Stir up one of the parts properly and pour it into a cauldron and light a fire under the cauldron. When the woad begins to boil, stir it, though not too vigorously, yet carefully in order to prevent the woad sinking and destroying the cauldron. If the woad separates it has been heated as it should be. Remove the fire, but do not stop stirring the woad. Now put in half a *choimix* (1.1 lb or $\frac{1}{2}$ kilo) of soapwort. Lay the stems on the edge of the vessel, cover with mats and light a moderate fire under it, so that it is kept suitably warm. Leave it to stand for three days.

Boil up the urine with soapwort, skim it and put in washed wool. Then rinse properly, squeeze it out and then put it into the dye-bath. When it looks to be all right, remove the wool and cover the dye-bath again. Make a bath of two *Minen* (*c.*2.2 lb or 1 kilo) of Orsellic, boil it up and skim. Place the dyed wool in this. Rinse in salt water and allow it to cool.

The soil best suited for woad is sand and sand-mould, and what it prefers is exposure to sea-air and wind. In marshy ground the leaves turn yellow and the entire plant does not thrive. The most suitable time to sow it is September in the autumn, or else in spring in the middle of April. In this way woad can be brought to yield three good harvests a year. When the woad leaves are about 5 inches (c. 12 cm) broad and half an ell long (c.1' or 30 cm) at the same time as the tips of the leaves or edges have yellowed, the woad is ripe for harvesting.

Large plantations of woad call for a special woad-mill for crushing the woad leaves. The mill that I had built here in Åbo (has as) its great advantage (...) that it can be sited in one and the same house in which the woad is prepared. It can be driven without horses or men, only by children ten or twelve years of age.

Once the woad has been crushed in the mill, the woad-makers of Erfurt and Thuringia stack it in a pile for a whole day to allow the woad's sap to strain off. After that the woad is squeezed with the hands into balls as large as a man's fist. These are dried on specially constructed drying racks. After 14 to 20 days these woad-balls are usually so dry that they can be piled up and stored for future selling. Properly prepared woad-balls can be kept for eight to ten years without deteriorating. They can be used for dyeing as soon as they are dry.

Other indigo-yielding plants

A large number of plants that yield indigo, other than indigo and woad, grow all over the world. There has scarcely been a civilisation using textiles that did not have this valuable dye. The most important seems to have been *Polygonum tinctoria*. This has been used in China and Japan since long back in time and has been grown experimentally in Germany and France. Perhaps less well known is the fact that a blue dye can be made from weld (*Reseda lutesia*). Normally this is used in conjunction with a mordant to produce yellows that are relatively fast. In 18th-century France various varieties of weld were grown in France and other places partly for yellow dyeing and partly for blue dyeing. A dyer's book of 1772 contains a chapter entitled 'How weld-bath is to be prepared', in which it is stated that the 'weld-bath is to be prepared in the same way as the woad-bath and thus there is little or nothing more to be said about it. The only difference between the two is that weld is weaker and does not give so much colour. . . .'

The import of indigo to Europe really got going with the discovery of the Sea Road to India round the Cape of Good Hope in 1498. Modest in the early days, in the first half of the 16th century when a regular trade had been established, it grew and grew.

Although indigo yields a dye that in many respects is undoubtedly superior and many times stronger than, for example, woad, its import was for a long time a considerable gamble. This was due to a strongly protectionist resistance to it in most countries where cultivation of woad was a significant industry, as it was especially in central Europe. It was not only important to the dyers, but also, and perhaps even more important, was its contribution to a state's revenues through taxation. Thus the opposition of the woad-growers was naturally supported by their governments, which sought to protect their own economic structure by prohibiting the use of indigo. Thus, in France in 1598, the use of indigo was forbidden and a number of drastic laws and decrees were also issued. For example, dyers had to swear an oath that they would not use indigo, but confine themselves to woad. In Nürnberg, they were threatened with death if the law was not obeyed. The sale of textiles dyed with indigo was also strictly forbidden.

England, unlike the Continent, had never had any significant production of woad.

Now, its interests were centred more and more on the products of the countries of its Empire, especially India, where the British traders of the early 17th century gave indigo pride of place among the exports of the Orient.

Thus towards the end of the 17th century, when the Dutch started a well-organised trade in tropical products: silk, spices and dye-stuffs, this inevitably led to indigo making the final breakthrough. The ban on it was lifted and for the next couple of centuries it was to be in Europe, as well as elsewhere, the indispensable and best of all dyes.

An engraving from Pehr Adrian Gadd's *Färge-stoften Veides plantering och Ans i Finland* (The cultivation and care of the dye-stuff Woad in Finland), 1760.

Blue woad is produced and used in roughly the same manner as indigo. The difference between woad and Asiatic indigo is that the dye-element in woad is considerably less concentrated and results in yellow dye-stuff which tends to break the fibres at the same time as the result is a more indistinct, greenish tinge on the material.

When, during the Napoleonic wars, the Continental blockade stopped the import into the Continent of goods from outside, interest in woad revived. Rich rewards were promised to those able to improve the methods of its cultivation and its use in dyeing so as to make it competitive with indigo. Napoleon himself promised Fr. 425,000 for this purpose.

In the picture above:

A. Fields of woad; B. Basal rosette ready for harvesting; C. woad sickle; D. tank in which the harvested leaves are fermented; E. woad mill; F. Balls of woad; G. Drying frame for woad balls; H. woad-mass (moistened with water); I. tank for storing the woad dye-stuff; K. woad bath (for dyeing); L. Plant with its leaves and flowers; M. Woad-plant with seed-pods; N. a ripe seed.

NATURAL INDIGO – SYNTHETIC INDIGO

A Strife with Global Consequences

While in the first half of the 17th century indigo was hedged about with restrictions and prohibitions, and called by those who disliked it, a 'Devil's Dye', by the end of that century indigo had become prized and indispensable. Its victory in the West was as dramatic and exciting as any tale of adventure, a fascinating chapter of man's history, in which selfishness and the lust for gain had to yield to the demands of common sense and practicality.

The great geographical discoveries of the 15th and 16th centuries led to the establishment of *direct* trading links with India and Indonesia for all goods from East Asia. The new sea routes, together with new designs for bigger and better ships, caused the traditional old Silk Road and the equally ancient traffic along the coasts of the Mediterranean to lose almost all their importance as links between East and West. Instead, big powerful ships, so called 'East Indiamen', crisscrossed the oceans laden with silk, porcelain, spices and cases of indigo.

The actual voyages were fraught with risks of misadventure and attack; and the ships in which they were made had to be of extra stout construction, have large crews and be fitted with adequate armament. The first expedition sent by the Dutch East India Company lasted from April 1595 to August 1597, and the first of those of the British East India Company from May 1601 to September 1603, which shows how long and risky these voyages were.

Such expeditions were enormously costly and to finance them people formed themselves into trading companies which were granted certain privileges in their home countries. The oldest and most important of these was the British East India Company which was formed in 1600, and it was followed two years later by a Dutch company. These voyages generally brought rich returns, up to 50 per cent after repayment of a capital put up separately for each voyage.

The demand for indigo in Europe increased every year and the size of the plantations in British India increased correspondingly, as did those in Java and the islands of the Caribbean. Trade in tropical products began to assume gigantic proportions, and the shrewd placed their capital in the Bengal Indigo Corporation of Calcutta or in another of the mighty East India companies.

The early 19th century gave out hope of continued expansion and development of the technology of both textiles and dyeing. As imports grew, new dye-stuffs emerged: quercitron, sandalwood and others, but where blue was concerned indigo remained supreme. There were no clouds on the horizon, and the rumours that cropped up

every now and then of the new chemical industry experimenting with the production of new dye-stuffs, were dismissed as wishful thinking on the part of traditionally optimistic researchers. But ironically enough it was just in that area that things were happening.

The years that followed were full of new ideas, confidence in the future and the desire to experiment. Nature with all it had to offer was no longer frightening and inaccessible. Man was all set to master it and extort from it its resources for the benefit and well-being of everyone. The whole century was influenced by this dynamic materialistic attitude, which was not to be critically revised and diverted into other channels until our own day.

Technical development now began to bring about social change in various areas and to an extent that had not previously been experienced. Lighting, for example, became a subject of radical change. Forms

An East Indiaman.

Cargoes of silk-stuffs from China, cotton materials and dye-stuffs from India and spices from Indonesia were brought back to Europe in big, powerful sailing ships, known as East Indiamen.

31

of lighting had changed but insignificantly through the ages. The difference between a flaring torch, an oil lamp or a wax candle was minimal. But at the turn of the century, around 1800, gas for lighting was on the way and soon to be in common use in all bigger towns and cities in Europe. It was produced by heating coal, which also produced coke for heating dwellings and the manufacture of industrial raw materials, as well as a third product, coal-tar. This was a black, sticky mass that was nothing but a source of unpleasantness, whose disposal posed a considerable problem.

In the 1830s an eminent chemist and medical doctor, Ferdinand Runge, was busily engaged trying to discover a practical use for this evil-smelling, undesirable byproduct of the gas industry, which was rapidly accumulating in tanks in the gas works of Berlin, where he worked. In 1834 he succeeded in isolating one of coal-tar's compounds: anilin oil. Aniline was already known, as it had been produced in breaking down indigo. The idea that it might be possible to produce a dye-stuff from similar oil was, according to Runge, a logical follow up. Indeed, he succeeded, using oxidisation of the oil, in producing various different dyestuffs, one of which was a blue. However, no one yet suspected what those first tentative experiments would lead to. The management of the works thwarted Runge in the most shameful manner, for example by preventing the results of his experiment being given to the directors. Runge's skilful and systematic experiments might otherwise have led in a relatively short time to the decisive discovery of the nature of this aromatic coal compound and so have provided him with the key to the whole of organic chemistry.

Instead, in the middle of the 19th century, a young chemist's daring experiment fundamentally changed the dye industries of England and the rest of the world. The chemist was William Perkin, an eighteen-year-old laboratory assistant working with Professor Hofmann at the Royal College of Chemistry in London. He used his spare time trying to produce quinine (for use against malaria) synthetically. One of his experiments, in which he used aniline as his base, left him with an indeterminate blue mass in his retort, and from this, after some protracted laboratory work, he succeeded in isolating a violet dye-stuff that was to be called mauvein. Perkin's daring idea that quinine could be produced from aniline came to nothing, but, instead, he had produced the first serviceable tar dye-stuff The year 1850 is usually regarded as being the year in which the tar dye industry was born.

Researchers in this new area of experiment were fully aware that henceforth the chemistry of dyes was a question of 'building up', a form of architecture. Earlier, in *inorganic* chemistry which dealt mainly with metals and combinations of metals, the most important thing had been to discover of which base elements a certain substance was comprised. With this so-called 'gross formula' one could go on to determine the integral substances. But in *organic* chemistry, the question is *how* the different atoms in a molecule are linked. Thus the structure of the element was the important thing. This provided a sort of plan of how the various atoms of carbon, hydrogen and oxygen were combined (see page 136).

A page from *Technische Chemie* by Ferdinand Runge, 1838.

The pattern of the sample of material dyed with indigo illustrated on this page was obtained by using a resist-paste containing zinc-nitrate.

From primeval forest to dye-stuff

Organic chemistry has often been referred to as the chemistry of carbon compounds and, indeed, the basic material for this new science is the coal-tar about which we have been talking. This being so, one is entitled to say that the roots of the chemistry of dyes go back hundreds of millions of years to the so-called carboniferous age, a fact that one does not always remember when you are standing weighing out and mixing the dyes for a bath; but it is indeed a fact that the basic material for one's powder was formed some 300 million years ago.

Earth's climate then was warm and moist and there were no real changes of season. This gave rise to huge primeval forests of tall tree-like horsetails and ferns among other growth. Alternating volcanic eruptions and earthquakes time and again buried the forests beneath layers of mud and gravel, causing the vegetable matter to undergo a chemical change induced first by bacteria and then by the pressure of the overlying mass of earth and by the heat, thus making them poorer in hydrogen and oxygen and consequently richer in carbon. For millions of years these forests, now turned to coal, lay undisturbed in the earth's interior. It was not till the early days of organic chemistry that they were brought back up to the surface, studied and made to appear in new and quite different forms, for example as dyes of superb quality and great variety. At the same time as chemists were endeavouring to create new dyes, great efforts were made to discover the composition of the old natural dyes so that the new techniques might be able to produce them artificially.

Because of its dominant position, indigo had always tempted researchers, but it long resisted all attempts to determine its chemical structure as, indeed, did madder. In 1808 two researchers succeeded in determining the constitution of alizarin which is the active compound of madder-root. Not long afterwards, A. von Bayer, the renowned German chemist who had earlier determined the constitution of indigo, produced the first synthetic indigo. Further work on the problem enabled it to be handed over to Badische Anilin Soda Fabrik and production began. In 1897 BASF introduced the first artificial indigo onto the market.

Meanwhile there had been no lack of protests about the new research, its results and expected significance. In the early summer of 1862 a big international technical exhibition was held which was attended by scientists from all over the world. The opening speech was made by William Perkin's teacher, Professor Hofmann, and in it he told his audience that before long England would have become the main dye-producing country in the world; that she would even be sending blue dyes made from coal to indigo-producing India. . . . Here, to the horror of his audience, he was interrupted by an old man, who had thrust his way up to the rostrum. This disturber of the peace was James Mansfield, spokesman of the British and Dutch indigo syndicates. In considerable agitation he described the ruinous consequences to British world trade, if the professor's prediction should prove true. His audience sat dumbfounded that anyone should have interrupted the official speaker in the presence of the Queen and so distinguished a company. Such a thing had never happened before. Professor Hofmann, however, took it all perfectly calmly. Perhaps he was thinking of his friend and collaborator, Charley Mansfield, who had been killed in an explosion at a factory producing dyes, while working on the new dyes, and who had been the son of the man in front of him.

Production of synthetic indigo was now in full swing and it was prophesied that it would swiftly and dramatically alter trading relations in Europe, with knock-on effects wherever in the world indigo was an important product. In 1895–96 India exported some 18,700 tons of indigo, but in 1913–14 the figure had shrunk to only 1,000 tons. Soon after that India began importing synthetic indigo. At roughly the same time Germany had imported natural indigo to the value of 20 million marks, yet in 1913–14 it was, instead, exporting its own indigo to the value of over 50 million marks. The great indigo syndicates answered the new threat by reducing prices drastically, but the synthetic product was well able to counter every such manoeuvre and within a few years of its appearance on the market, natural indigo had lost its world preeminence and a few decades later the industry was almost wholly destroyed.

Synthetic indigo had several advantages: it contained fewer impurities than did natural indigo; the colour was constant; and its manufacture was not affected by capricious weather conditions.

Some people remained unaffected by the strife and new developments the new substance had caused: the Meo people of northern Thailand continued to dye their lengths of batik cloth with indigo, as did the Toba of northern Sumatra their dark-blue ikat cloth and the Yoruba women of West Africa their paste-treated adire fabrics as they had done since days so distant that none had any idea of their craft's beginnings.

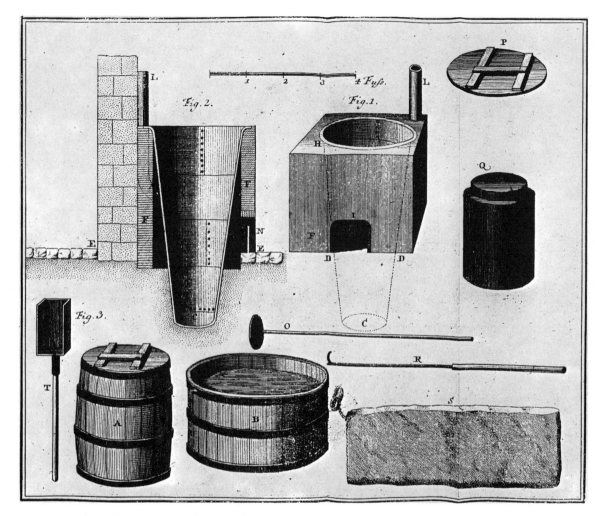

Equipment for a 'blueing-room' illustrated in *Die Kunst der Seidenfärberey* by P. J. Macquer, 1759.

In former times every dye-works of any size had a special room for dyeing with indigo and woad, a so-called 'blueing-room'. This was regarded as the holy of holies of the dye-house and as a rule only the dye-master himself and his immediate assistants might enter it.

In the picture reproduced here can be seen some of the most characteristic tools and equipment used in the blueing-room: first and foremost the large hot-bath (Fig. 1) which was the most important part of the room. It had a deep copper lining which was partly sunk into the ground; the upper part being bricked round with flues which generated the heat. A section of the hot-bath (Fig. 2) shows the depth of the vat which could be as great as 13' (4 m with a width of 6½'–8' (2–2.5 m). Of the tools depicted O is the 'soaker' which was used for stirring and which could be as long as 4 metres; R is the 'bath-hook' with its wooden handle and iron claw for manoeuvring the material during the dyeing process. Delicate materials (other than silk) were kept in a pouch of loosely woven material, S, while they were being dyed.

DYEING AND PRINTING WITH INDIGO

About Dye-works and Using Dyes in Olden Days

The technique used in dyeing must always be suited to both the kind of fibre being dyed and the dye-stuff being used. Mordant dyes, which constitute the largest group of dyeing substances, adhere to animal fibres without any complicated equipment or procedure, while they have considerably greater difficulty in dyeing vegetable materials. Substantive or non-mordant dyes (indigo and purple) on the other hand, though they use different methods, will dye all kinds of fibre, but in return require a certain amount of technical equipment and a considerable amount of knowledge and experience on the part of those who use them. This led to the development as long ago as in antiquity of a special profession, that of dyeing with indigo and, for a certain limited time, of purple-dyeing too; while dyeing using other dyes was undertaken by the textile makers themselves In many parts of the world this division still persists, though the northern countries to a certain extent provide the exception. Even after proper dye-works were established the country people of the North dyed with the various substantive dyes (birch leaf, black alder bark, roots of *Galium boreale* etc.) as well as some form of indigo. The evidence for this lies in the wealth of instruction and recipe books published in those countries in the 18th and 19th centuries.

Two important requirements had to be met before a dye-works could be set up in any particular place: first, that there was a good supply of fire-wood available for heating the dye-bath and the water for washing and rinsing; then the proximity of a stream, brook or river with water of good quality. This last was particularly important, because, if the water contained too much organic matter, that could impart a yellowish tinge to the yarn and fabric; or, if it contained iron, that darkened all bright tones; or again, if it was so-called hard water, containing calcium, it made it unsuitable for dyeing with indigo, because of its tendency to precipitate the dye-stuff dissolved in the bath.

Let me quote from Jean Hellot's *Dyers bible* of the 1770s:

> So not just any water can be best for different dyes, nor any one kind of water for all dyes, for one water can be suitable for one colour, but harmful for another, and that a Master should understand, so these craftsmen must investigate the different kinds of water and learn about them. One should not imagine that the small amount of matter in water is of no significance. This matter can at times spoil the entire dye.

Every dye-works, big or little, had to have two separate areas: one larger and more spacious for 'colour dyeing' with all the many vats and vessels required and arrangements for dyeing with substantive dyes of different kinds. Then a smaller, though perhaps more important area, the 'blueing-room' where fermentation-vat dyeing with indigo and woad was carried out. It was important that it should be possible to have a good through draught in this area in order to speed up the process of oxidisation in the dyed yarn or cloth. One further room was needed, a drying-room or attic arranged for the type of goods the works processed. Larger dye-works could also have space for fulling, dressing, shearing and some form of textile printing, usually with blue.

In the larger room were a number of dye-pans or vats, each for a special purpose, grouped round a large brick furnace. The largest vat, which would be some 1.3 cu. yd. (2 m³) in volume, was used for dyeing homespun and other cloths brown and black. The smaller vats were used for different coloured dyes and the smallest were for silk and trying out new colours or dyes.

A dye-works was divided in accordance with the two main types of dye: substantive vat-dyes and mordant dyes. The blueing-room was equipped and arranged in accordance with the kinds of fibres that were going to be dyed there. If it was a question of

An engraving from Macquer's book of 1759 showing the interior of a dye-works. A number of different activities are illustrated: an assistant is using rods to turn a quantity of cloth in the

dye-bath (A). In the middle of the room another assistant is busy threading hanks of yarn onto rods preparatory to dyeing (C); at (E) surplus solution is being wrung out of the yarn with the aid of a so-called 'doll'. Among the tools on the right of the picture is, at the top, a stretcher on which the dyed material is taken to the landing-stage by the river.

woollen materials, the dominant feature of the room was the so-called 'hot-bath'. This consisted of a large copper pan in the shape of a truncated cone, about 10′–13′ (3–4 m) deep and with a width of 6½′–8′ (2–2.5 m) at the top, tapering to 20″–29″ (0.5–0.75 m) at the bottom. This vat was buried for two-thirds of its length in the ground, the upper third being encased within a brick wall with a furnace whose flames reached the lowest part. At the conclusion of the dyeing the vat was covered with a lid made of two semi-circular parts. In the roof above the hot-bath was placed a large iron hook on which the dyed homespun could be hung for the solution to be squeezed out of it before it was taken to be cooled, aired and folded into lengths a yard or metre wide. Close to the hot-bath there would always be the bath-crown, a round rim of iron covered with a stout netting which was lowered into the bath in order to prevent the material being dyed touching the dregs in the bottom.

Cotton and linen materials were dyed in so-called 'cold-baths', consisting of oaken vats as tall as a man or even old wine-barrels with the bottoms knocked out and the bung-hole plugged. Dye-works which went in for some form of resist patterning (except blue-printing) would have a number of cement tanks sunk into the floor, each large enough for breadths of cloth to be immersed in it full length. Even for these some kind of bath-ring was needed to prevent the cloth touching the sediment on the bottom. The cold of the ground helped to keep the bath at the 68–75°F (20–24°C) most suitable for dyeing cotton, despite changes of temperature in other parts of the works.

The equipment of the blueing-room contained various characteristic tools (not needed elsewhere), among them the 'bloom-rake' used to remove the 'bloom' on the surface of the liquor in the bath before dyeing, and also the 'bloomboard' used to retain the raked bloom at one edge of the bath during dyeing; then there was the 'bath-hook', an iron tool with a wooden handle used for working the material under the surface of the solution; then there was the 'bath-stretcher' on which the dyed material was loaded and so taken down to the river for rinsing. The well-equipped dye-works would also have a large iron mortar for crushing larger chunks of indigo and a copper brayer for pulverising and 'creaming' the indigo.

The vessels of various shapes and sizes used in dyeing with indigo have traditionally been called 'baths'. One form of indigo-bath that was long used was the so-called 'fermentation-bath' in which the dye-stuff was made soluble in water with the help of micro-organisms and alkaline substances such as lime and lye. The bacteria, whose metabolism produced the required reduction, were often assisted with some food-stuff that enhanced their effect, such as sugar, honey, molasses etc. Since a fermentation-bath can only be achieved and kept 'alive' at a temperature of 104°F (40°C), it has usually been called a 'hot-bath'.

One special form of fermentation-bath that has been used for thousands of years is the 'urine-bath', in which the bacteria are able both to dissolve the dye-stuff and create a satisfactory alkaline environment for the dissolved indigo. From the technical point of view the urine-bath is an excellent method of dyeing, being relatively easy to look after and very kind to the material being dyed, usually wool. A recipe for such a bath dating from 1762 is reproduced on page 171.

During the 19th century new types of dissolving dye-stuffs were developed enabling reduction to take place with the help of different chemical substances. After this the dye-bath no longer needed to be kept hot, which was of great advantage for the more usual forms of resist-printing. These new

Scarves. That on the left is a resist-print (blueprint) from Austria, the work of Josef Koó, senior; that on the right is from Dalecarlia in Sweden and done by the ikat technique.

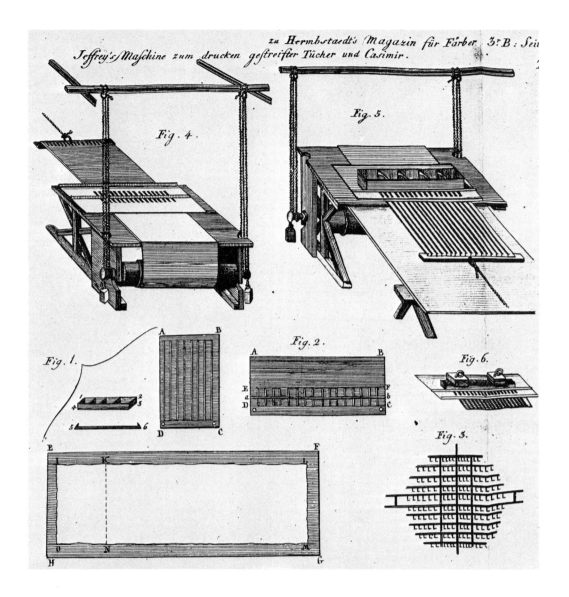

Fig. 4.

Fig. 5.

Fig. 1.

Fig. 2.

Fig. 6.

Fig. 3.

Engraving from *Magazin für Färber*, 1804.

In the latter half of the 18th century textile printers in England and France employed an ingenious machine that was able mechanically to apply a resist to cloth. It was used for both woollen and linen materials and the paste it employed was composed of pipe-clay and tallow or even beeswax.

versions of dye-bath, specially suited for vegetable fibres, were called 'cold-baths'. The term included lime-vitriol and oxide of common calamine baths. Recipes and instructions for cold-baths can be found on pages 129 and 156.

The hydrogen sulphite bath which was developed towards the end of the 19th century dyed both wool and cotton and even though the methods have to be adapted to some extent to the kind of fibre, this implied a considerable simplification of the vat process with the difficulties of management.

Preparing a bath called for knowledge and long experience and this meant that it was mostly the master himself who performed it, while the lesser employees were engaged on other tasks. Dyers themselves considered managing the hot-bath the most difficult to learn of all the tasks of their profession. A Swedish writer's book on the Vollsjö dye-works describes how 'the big bath sometimes behaved, despite all precautions, like an hysterical old-person, stubbornly persisting in refractoriness and malevolence. Thus there were good grounds for the old saying that "the dye-bath was the dyer's strictest master".'

In olden times there can scarcely have been a dyer who understood the chemical processes that took place during dyeing, but those who had long worked in the profession will certainly have accumulated a fund of experience and knowledge that was not to be despised. Using his hand he could judge whether the bath was at the right temperature, and his nose told him whether or not it required to be 'sharpened', that is for a little more lime to be added. By scrutinising the surface of the liquor, the blue-violet iridescent bubbles of the bloom could tell him the state of the indigo before the day's dyeing.

Printing with indigo

The deep-blue fast indigo-dye tempted the textile printers of 18th-century Europe to experiment with applying it to cotton material in some direct procedure: block-printing or painting on with a brush. The desire to be able to produce patterns with graceful delicate blue designs on a light or white background had long been there among the dyers of India and Indonesia. Despite their high, indeed hitherto unequalled, expertise, they had never succeeded in solving the problems of direct printing, but instead had gone in for resist (wax and resin) and piece-dyeing in a cold-bath. There are examples of British pattern-orders being sent to India for execution in

which as much as 90 per cent of the material's surface was covered before dyeing, so as to have the desired blue against a light background. In 1730 it was thought that a solution had been found. This entailed adding arsenic-trisulphide when printing so as to prolong the process of oxidisation for the necessary period. This method, originally developed so that the indigo could be applied with a brush, was thus called 'brush-blue'. This dye was appallingly dangerous to the health of those who used it and was soon replaced by other, less noxious though technically inferior variants, such as faience and English blue.

Then in 1883 they succeeded in arriving at a method which seemed really promising. Using this, it was possible to produce a deep blue that was most attractive, but the drawback was that the whole process was extremely complicated and lengthy. This meant that dyers were reluctant to use it generally and so, when a few years later, the new synthetic blue dyes that were easy to apply came on the market, it too became unimportant.

'As the first of the sun's rays touched the fallow-land on the plateau, I reached the height with the indigo plants. The seed you once sowed has been transformed into verdant plants. In the afternoon I spin cotton in the shady coolness of our home. The strands of the cotton, longer than the clouds and the hills – are as white as the waterfall beside the town. In the evening I go back to my room, and the threads I had dyed with blue from the indigo plants you sowed, are transformed into a patterned scarf.... Mother asks me: "For whom is this beautifully woven scarf intended?" In the dusk I smile to myself and my glances go towards the north.'

From the poem of the Banar people from *Poèmes du Sud Vietnam.*

PATTERNING WITH INDIGO

Resist-paste

White design – blue background

It is possible to produce a simple design or a figurative picture composition on a textile base using different *direct* methods. For example, it can be achieved by painting a thickened dye-solution onto the cloth or by applying it with a stamp or stencil. For a very long time now this has also been done by using *indirect* methods: ikat, plangi and wax-batik being those that are best known.

As well as indigo-dyeing cloth in order to achieve a blue background, it is also possible to achieve white and coloured designs. Here, one can adopt two different methods: either one can print, paint or squirt a preparation that will prevent the blue dye from attaching to the fibres onto the cloth before it is dyed; or one can go the other way round and *destroy* the dye in those places where the design is wanted. This latter can be done, for example, by using a stamp to apply a 'mass' containing suitable chemical substances to the cloth that has already been dyed.

The preparation used to protect certain parts of the material from the dye-solution, or which contains the substances that will destroy the dye locally, is usually called a *paste*. If using the first method, we speak of it as resist- or protective-paste; in the case of the second method we speak of a discharge- or etching-paste. A paste can be so composed that it protects the cloth from the effect of the indigo solution at the same time as it gives colour to the resist or protected parts of the design. It can also be made so as to protect against one dye, while allowing another to attach.

In the West, the production of cloth using

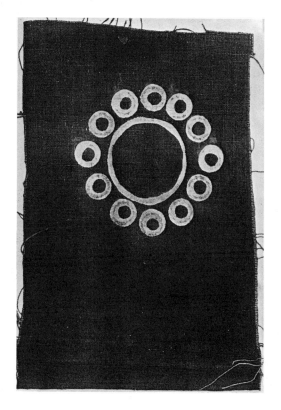

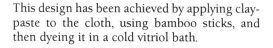

This design has been achieved by applying clay-paste to the cloth, using bamboo sticks, and then dyeing it in a cold vitriol bath.

Fragment of an Indian banner, resist-patterned, found in Fustat, near Cairo. It was probably made in Gujarat about 1000–1500 AD. Its colours are indigo-blue and white, the material cotton. The resist was probably wax and resin.

resist-pastes is usually called 'blue-printing', a term that is used even when it is not just a question of having a white design on a blue background. When you first hear the expression 'blue-print', you naturally assume it to refer to a blue design on a light or white background; i.e. the application, by printing, of a blue dye onto the surface of a textile material. But in actual fact it is the other way round: the protective substance – the resist-paste – is imprinted onto the cloth on just those places which are to take the design. After dyeing, the protected paste produces a white design against a blue background. To call this blue-printing is thus quite misleading.

The production of designs by means of resist-pastes and indigo-dyeing is considered to be the oldest method of decorating textiles. This view is strengthened by the fact that in India cotton cloth decorated with a combination of resist-painting and resist-printing were being produced long before the start of the Christian era. Clay, resin and wax may well have been used.

During excavations in Fustat (old Cairo) quantities of Indian printed materials were found, which are considered to have been produced in Gujarat on the west coast of India and from there exported westwards by sea through the Red Sea to Egypt and so to Fustat. Marco Polo, who visited the kingdoms that later constituted the province of Gujarat, wrote admiringly of the many coloured cotton materials and gossamer-thin veils that were manufactured there.

The colours of the cloth found at Fustat are exclusively indigo-blue, madder-red and white (the material's basic colour). The design has been produced by an early, perhaps the original, resist-technique, by means of which the lines, dots etc. of the design stand out white on a coloured or dark background. Later Indian prints used a black-brown colour instead and delicate designs which also served as a base for the application of resist-, discharge- and colouring-pastes (see page 106).

What has been said so far shows how patterning with a resist-paste and an indigo-bath had reached a high degree of perfection as early as several thousand years ago. But how it began, where it began and why it began are things at which we can only guess. In writing this book which has sought to describe the processes and conditions of very distant times, the writer has often had to venture into the uncertain ground of conjecture and must do so here, if any of those questions are to be answered. It would be helpful if one were to accept that progress in dyeing technology has been due far less to systematic innovation and experiment than to clever observation when mistakes have been made and chance results in the actual process of dyeing, which were then developed into new ways that could be applied in practice.

Different pastes

The technique of using a protective coat of some kind must have originated at a time when all tasks were performed in close proximity to each other. Clay, for example, was early used both for building and for making household utensils. One can see how splashes of clay on a cloth were seen to cause white specks or patches when that cloth was dyed. Clays have also been used in all ages as a resist in the production of blue-print alone or in combination with other materials. Wax is another substance that has been largely used in different cultures as a preserving and protecting layer on painted surfaces of wood or plaster. Resin is another protective and resist-material, its qualities early showing, perhaps involuntarily, that it was superbly capable of resisting even the strongest indigo solution. Later it was to become one of the most important compounds of Indian pastes used in printing textiles, as well as of Javanese wax-resists.

The worldwide spread of resist techniques, not least in the production of blue-print, was due in part to the fact that the substances required for this protective layer were to be found practically everywhere. The same thing goes for the dye that made the technique serviceable – indigo. This favourable circumstance has contributed to the fact that the production of the different forms of blue-print became an 'everyday art' in the true sense of the words.

One might suppose that because of its apparently simple method of patterning and its use of one colour – blue – all resist-printing should look pretty well alike wherever it was produced. On the contrary, the wealth of variation here is astounding. Of course, as in all craft production, it is the local conditions in the guise of material and technical resources, social and cultural factors etc. which play a sometimes decisive part.

After blue-printing, the design should stand out as clearly and distinctly as possible from the background. The extent to which this is possible depends largely on the composition of the protective layer and the way in which it is applied to the cloth.

Technically, a resist-paste can act in two different ways: either purely *mechanically* in that its impermeability prevents the indigo penetrating into the fibres, which thus remain uncoloured. Or it can have a *chemical* action through having in its composition substances that form impenetrable deposits in the paste when the cloth is immersed in the alkaline bath. The composition of an efficient paste is based on the choice of its components and the relationship between them, changing in accordance with the strength of the bath and the intensity of the blue that it is wanted to resist.

European pastes almost without exception contain added ingredients which enhance the protective action and sometimes also have colouring qualities of their own. These are what we call chemical pastes. The Asiatic, and to some extent the African pastes as well, are usually purely 'mechanical' and consist mainly of flour, starch, wax, resin or clay.

The Chinese early developed a paste composed of ground soya bean and slaked lime. This covered extremely well and allowed the dyeing of deep shades of blue. Blue-printing was then exported to Japan, where the method was modified so as to meet certain local requirements. For example, soya-flour was replaced by rice-flour and rice-husks as the principal ingredient. This paste was obtained from finely ground 'sticky' rice which adhered firmly to the fibres whatever the method of applying it. This rice-paste permits the reproduction of the finest lines and, once dry, it will stand up to the indigo-liquor being painted on, or even its immersion in a dye-bath. As well as rice-flour the Japanese paste contains lime and salt.

The Yoruba people of West Africa have long been famous for their dynamically vital resist-patterned *adire* cloth. Literally, *adire* means 'knotted and dyed', but it has come to be used for all indigo-dyed material from Yoruba-land. One form of adire, *adire-eleko*, employs a paste that is painted onto the cloth with a brush or feather, or can also be applied using a sheet-stencil perforated with the design. The ingredients of the paste vary slightly from district to district, but it consists mainly of cassava-root flour (starch) mixed with water. In a number of places yam-flour is added and also a little blue vitriol, the purpose of which is to help to keep the paste fresh for as long as possible. The paste is removed after dyeing, but some starch is always left in the cloth which gives it a certain stiffness when it is dried.

Indonesia, especially the island of Java, is famous for the production of batik, in which a wax-hard resist is applied to the cloth by means of a copper stamp. Other forms of resist and other methods of applying them existed earlier, but opinions are divided as to their origins and use. In one of these original methods of patterning, katjang-batik, a paste of soya-flour was used. It was applied to both sides of the cloth using stencils made of lacquered paper. Such materials were produced in large quantities in the middle of the 19th century in western Java. The method used is thought to have been introduced by the Chinese who had long used a very similar process for their blue-prints.

We have emphasised the basic differences between the European, often complicated *chemical* pastes and the Asiatic *mechanical*, protective pastes. The difference between these two resist types becomes even greater when we consider the method used for applying them to the actual textiles. While the Europeans have made exclusive use of the old block-printing method, in China and Japan, for example, it was the stencil that was the favourite tool.

When, during the 17th and 18th centuries, the blue-dyers of Europe began to supplement their activities with blue-printing, they were often able to take over the printing-blocks used in earlier textile printing with, say, oil-based pigments. The old matrices with raised designs cut out of the wood were gradually modified to make them respond better to the special requirements of blue-printing. Perhaps the most important of these was that the individual parts of the design must be relatively small and evenly divided over the surface to be covered. One can see how the blocks of the end of the 19th and the early 20th centuries, the heyday of the blue-print, had been adapted to this technique by the use of metal pins and thin brass strips.

In China and Japan wooden stamps were being used very early on, as has been shown by various fragments of cloth that have been preserved. Gradually, however, they were replaced by stencils made of stout, specially prepared rice-paper strengthened with silken gauze. These did not soften, even when subjected to lengthy wetting, and offered, above all, a considerably larger printing surface than wooden-blocks could offer. This rice-paste was applied with a small, thin, pliable wooden scraper. It had to be applied to both sides of the material, since both the Chinese and the Japanese liked to have both back and front the same. The oldest Japanese resist-stencilled cloth that has survived dates back to the 14th century and is of such high quality that one must assume that they had mastered the technique long before then.

Blue-print in Europe

Resist-printing is a late phenomenon in Western textile crafts. It developed naturally enough in time with the increase in the use of Asiatic indigo and the (new) opportunity for dyeing vegetable fibres by means of the cold-bath, the latter of which is a prerequisite for producing blue-print.

The new patterning technique found favour above all in Central Europe. People, especially the country people, had always been restricted to undyed materials for their clothes and other textiles. Blue-print provided a product that was both extremely fast, durable and capable of great variety. It could be used for clothes, just as well as for furnishings. Its popularity was increased by the fact that it could be made relatively cheaply. Before long every town or large village in such countries as Poland, Bohemia, Hungary, and also Germany and Austria, had its own blue-dyer. The people of Moravia and Slovakia were renowned for the different forms of indigo-resist they employed. One original method employed in Tarnów, near the Polish border, and called metlíčkova, consisted of using a small broom or whisk to spatter the mixture of flour on lengths of linen before dyeing them blue. The cloth with this 'spatter pattern' was used for making the aprons that were part of the local women's dress.

From Josef Koó's dye-works in Steinberg.
The lengths of cloth overprinted with paste are hung up on poles in a room in the workshop for a couple of months, so that they can dry and/or harden.

My friend the blue-dyer

Gone now are the days when such as Alenka would go down to the blue-dyer's house by the river to order cloth for the skirt she was to wear for Sunday mass. This was a pleated skirt of dark-blue material with white sprigs of roses and it lasted a lifetime. Gone, too, are the blue-dyers with their craft that once was part of life in the small towns and villages of central-southern Europe. There is an old German expression that someone is 'as clever as a blue-dyer', and indeed they needed considerable intelligence to master the many problems which might confront such a craftsman in his daily work. A description of my friend Josef Koó, indigo-dyer and blue-printer of the Burgenland, will serve as a picture of the many clever, skilful and devoted dyers and printers who not all that long ago were to be found all over Europe, but of whom Josef and his wife, Elisabeth, are the last representatives.

Josef took over the little dye-works in Steinberg, near the frontier with Hungary, from his father to whom he had been apprenticed. The works consist of a collection of buildings with different functions clustered round a large yard, from which a dyer's walk leads down to the river.

The first building is that in which printing with resist-paste is carried out. In the middle stands a long printing table which is covered with a felt overlay to soften the contact between the block and the cloth material. The cotton material is spread out on the table and fixed down so that it cannot shift or be displaced during printing. Then, with a pencil, the main outline of the design is marked on the cloth. Sometimes the material is slightly dressed, which both makes printing easier and helps to induce a more even acceptance of the colour. A dash of blue vitriol in the starch is thought by many dyers to help, in that it gives a darker blue tone and causes the indigo to be absorbed more quickly. Often the cloth is mangled before being printed, especially when both sides are to be printed, as this helps to prevent the paste penetrating and causing a 'ghost pattern' on the other side.

On one of the short sides of the table is the 'stamp-pad' containing the paste. In its simplest form it consists of a cushion filled with potato-flour or stuffed with feathers and put in a low-sided drawer. The cushion is protected by an oiled overlay on which the requisite quantity of paste is poured. The paste is then spread with a wooden scraper until it forms an even layer of the right thinness. The block is pressed against the cushion and then quickly transferred to the area of the cloth that is to receive the paste. Josef strikes the block with five rhythmic powerful blows with clenched fists, so that the paste will adhere to the material underneath. Then, with a brisk movement he raises the stamp, replenishes the paste on it and so repeats the procedure until the whole length of cloth has been covered with its resist-pattern. The paste that Josef uses contains a filling such as kaolin and lead sulphate, a thickening medium such as gum arabic and some substances that form protective layers, such as copper or aluminium sulphate.

The majority of his printing stamps are between 100 and 150 years old and have been used before by Josef's father. Some have been taken over from other shops that have closed down. Almost all have metal pins and studs to provide finer detail in the design and raised parts in the wood for the cruder parts.

Stamp from Kitzbühl in Austria.

A printing block is often made of a hard wood such as pear, into which the design is incised or else carved out in relief. Finer details are provided by small metal pins or studs. In the back of the blocks are two grooves that provide a grip for the printer's hand and allow him to lift the stamp from the cloth or place it on it with precision.

51

The lengths of printed cotton are hung up on rods in the roof and are left up there for a couple of weeks while the paste dries. The actual dyeing starts with the cloth being fastened to the so-called star-frame, an iron frame with hooks in it which is hung on a chain over the dye-bath. The lid of the bath is taken off and the 'bloom' removed from the surface of the solution using a wooden rake and poured into a bucket by the side of the bath. After the dyeing is finished, it is poured back into the bath. Josef checks the composition of the bath, sharpening the contents if that should be necessary, and sometimes adding more indigo The star-frame with the lengths of cloth (which have to be dry) is lowered into the bath. The first dip lasts only five minutes, after which the cloth is lifted up above the surface and the oxygen in the air allowed to oxidise the dye for ten minutes. The next and subsequent dips last 20 minutes with intervals for oxidisation of 10 minutes Dyeing then continues until the material

has been dipped seven times and as many oxidisations have been allowed. Extreme dark shades call for even more immersions. A blue-black hue requires up to 12 or 15 immersions. It is an advantage if a good change of air can be provided for during oxidisation.

Josef uses a vitriol-lime bath, like that described on page 157. The dye-house houses three indigo baths of different sizes. These are large cement tanks some 13' (4 m) deep in which the requisite temperature of 68–75°F (20–24°C) is maintained throughout the entire dyeing season, which begins in March and continues until October.

Skirt and scarf of the costume of the women of Burgenland.

The skirt was printed by Josef Koó, senior, at the beginning of the 20th century. The colour, a deep blue-black, was obtained with a vitriol-lime bath and there is white resist-patterning.

Immediately after dyeing, the cloth has to be dried which is usually done outdoors or in a drying-room. It is not good to rinse the cloth immediately after dyeing, as this causes precipitation onto the white parts. The dried cloth is now 'soured' in a bath containing as much sulphuric acid as to give it a sour taste.

This treatment both enables the colour to stand up to rubbing and restores the whiteness of those parts of the design that the metal salts in the paste may have discoloured. During this process most of the paste is removed. Souring, washing and rinsing conclude the dyeing process. The cloth, dyed and dried, has to receive a last treatment before it is placed on shelves in the small store. This involves winding it onto powerful wooden rollers and putting it under the heavy upper-part of the big stone mangle as it goes to and fro, thereby giving the surface of the cloth a pretty gloss.

The production of blue-print is both complicated and costly in time and money. If the return is to be equivalent to the investment, blue-print necessarily becomes an expensive commodity. Substitutes and imitations produced by roller-print with etching paste have thus displaced blue-print in many places where it has long been produced, a change that makes one ask whether we have not lost something by replacing an age-old craft with a rational technologically excellent method of manufacture and, if we have, what? The resulting textiles look at first glance similar, but there is a catch here. There are a couple of not quite insignificant differences between the blue-print produced mechanically and that which is the product of craftsmanship. For many people these differences are most significant and decisive in their choice of cloth.

Cloth produced wholly mechanically obviously has a perfect, technically irreproachable appearance. All components of the pattern are identical and the whiteness of the

The pictures on pages 54–55 show:
a. Josef placing the lengths of cloth onto the hooks in the ring-frame
b. The cloth before immersion in the bath
c. The ring-frame being lowered into the bath
d. The cloth lifted out for the dye to be oxidised
e. The cloth being soured in a bath of sulphuric acid

Table cloth, 5′ × 6½′ (135 × 200 cm), printed by Josef Koó, junior.

A speciality introduced by Josef Koó's father in the 1920s was that of printing with blue on both sides of the material. During preparation the paste is applied to both sides by using printing-rollers. In this way you can produce cloth with a pattern border on one side and sprigs of flowers on the other side.

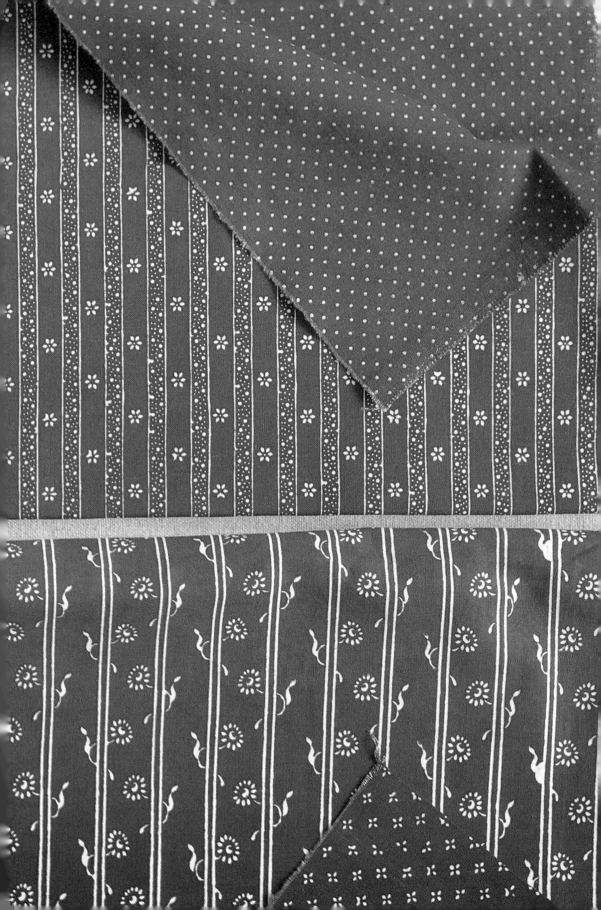

etched parts without discrepancy. But it is just this perfection that contains an element of danger. However cleverly the design is drawn, it loses its 'personality' due to the monotonous and uniform repetition due to the technique.

Where the cloth is a product of craft, the units of the printing-stamp are also repeated regularly across the surface, *but* however clever the printer is, slight variations inevitably occur. The outside edges of the stamp may, for example, not form an absolutely straight line, the connection between the impressions is not always perfect, the resistability of the paste is not always equally good throughout a design etc. All in all this results in tiny differences not always such as the eye can register, but which we do register mentally and that makes us feel the hand-made blue-print to be that much more alive and human.

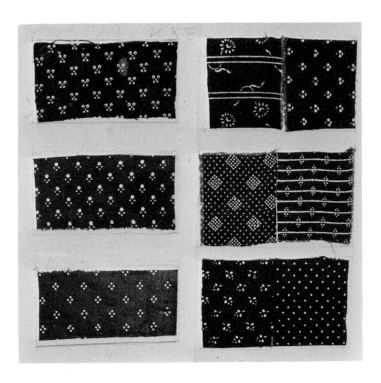

A page from a book of patterns belonging to Josef Koó, senior.

A blue-print patterned apron in the collection of
the Zorn Museum in Mora, Sweden.

West African Adire

Painted adire-eleko

In the previous chapter mention was made of the West African Yoruba people's form of resist-paste, *adire-eleko*. The starch-paste that provides the protective layer is either painted on with a brush, a feather or a stiff leaf-vein (from a palm leaf) or is applied by using a metal stencil.

The ingredients of the paste vary somewhat from district to district, but consist mainly of cassava root-flour mixed with water. The same kind of paste is used both for painting as for stencilling.

The basic lines of the design are obtained by folding the cotton material and this also gives the person with the brush certain guidelines for the subsequent work which is done completely without a pattern to follow. A plain strip of some 6″ (15 cm) wide is left at either end of the cloth to provide the hems. On one of these strips is placed the maker's signature or mark. This is almost always folded up under the hem, but, of course, is still there when the work is complete. The starch-paste is painted on so thickly that, when freshly put on, it stands up from the cloth, but subsequently part of it sinks into the cloth as it dries. A stroke or drop that by mistake lands on the cloth is swiftly removed with a pointed knife. The cloth, painted and ready, is carefully hung up on a bamboo pole to dry, a process that normally takes about three days, but if the atmosphere is damp, it can take longer. As soon as the cloth is quite dry, it is ready to be taken to the local dyer.

Most adire methods are specialities of their exponents. For example, all forms of plangi-patterning are done only by women, as is the exacting painting on of the paste, whereas the manufacture of the stencils and their printing is men's work. In Western Nigeria the dyeing is also women's work, while the concluding processes are performed by both men and women. In Northern Nigeria indigo dyeing is done solely by the men. It has a famous centre for dyeing in the town of Kano.

Among the Yoruba, those who carry out the dyeing have their own delineated area, in which several women can be found wor-

In the town of Kano in Northern Nigeria dyers still use the traditional stone-lined pits in the ground. Ismail, on the opposite page, is a foreman in one of the district's three dye-works.

king together. The huge pottery dye-pots are sunk into the ground and a low wall is built round them to provide the dyers with a seat which is sheltered by a simple straw roof, but if there are trees of any size in the immediate neighbourhood, the dyers will work under them. Everywhere are bamboo poles on which the dyed cloths are hung up to drip and dry. The ground round about is blue and the women who see to the drying have blue hands and often their feet are blue too. As dyeing is an hereditary craft, the apprentices who work with the dyers are all members of their families. However, dyeing is no longer an attractive job and today few want to take it up.

The blue dye used for adire-cloth is obtained from an indigo plant that is fairly common in Africa, *Lonchocarpus cyanescens*, known to the Yoruba as *elu-aja*, to the Hansa as *baba-rini* and to the Ibo as *uri*. Production varies from district to district, but follows the principles on which primitive indigo manufacture is based in many parts of the world.

Fresh green leaves of this bush are put in a large wooden mortar which has a heavy wooden pestle like those used for crushing corn. Once the leaves have been pounded into a blue-black mass, this is scraped together by hand and shaped into round lumps, which are left lying in the sun for two or three days. Those not needed for local use are collected in a basket or threaded on a cord, and taken to market to be sold.

Dyeing is always carried out in the shade, and the dye-bath is always kept well covered. A dyer will attend to five or six dye-baths at the same time. An ordinary bath requires some 50 indigo balls which are carefully crushed and covered with a lye solution of wood-ash to the requisite depth and this is then stirred. The bath is then left well-covered for some three days, before it is ready for use. During this time it has to be stirred at intervals. After three days blue bubbles will have formed on the surface and small bits of leaf have begun to float up, indicating that the bath is ready.

Different adire types call for different treatment in the bath. Plangi-pattern material can be immersed in the bath and cautiously squeezed with the hands. Painted and stencil-printed cloth must be treated differently, because if the paste were to be damaged, the dye would seep in and ruin the pattern. The cloth is folded up and carefully lowered into the bath, all the while being kept as level as possible, and there it stays for two or three minutes; it is then raised up and refolded so that the undyed parts are on the outside. This procedure is repeated until the whole of the cloth has received the dip that will give it the required shade. The cloth must be drip-dried before it can be rinsed and the paste removed. The last bit of treatment is for the cloth to be pounded with heavy wooden clubs until its surface is smooth and has acquired a matt sheen.

In Kano, the dyers' town of Northern Nigeria, they use cement dye-baths 10'–12' (3–4 m) deep, sunk into the ground and shaded with conical wicker shades. The dyers of Kano are notoriously great individualists and usually own the dye-baths which they work. They are often related. The liquor is prepared with lime, wood-ash and indigo as the main ingredients. After five days bubbles appear on the surface to show that fermentation is in progress. Long poles with a cross piece at one end are plunged into the bath and used to stir at intervals. When the bubbles are blue-violet and the liquor gives off a sweetish smell, dyeing can begin. People come to Kano from many different parts to have things dyed. It is to Kano that the Tuareg go to have headcloths dyed blue-black and their cloaks light-blue.

Adire cloth from Nigeria made by the stencil-resist process.

62

Karin Wallin, textile artist and teacher at
The Living Workshop, Stockholm: From
my diary, *January 1983*

'The everyday throng was a blue sea of
handmade indigo cloth against brown skin.
In towns such as Abeokuta, Ibadan
Oshogbo even the reddish brown earth was
dyed blue in the places where the women
dyers worked, for everywhere was dripping
cloth hung up to dry.'

This, though, is how Betty Okuboyejo, a
Scottish girl married in Nigeria, paints her
picture of the blue Yoruba land she encountered when she first came to south-western
Nigeria in the beginning of the 1960s: 'Our
encounter was rather different. We have
been here six weeks now and in all that time
we have seen only three people dressed in
indigo. The Nigerian throng in today's villages and towns is a colourful textile confu-

sion of Indonesian influenced patterns, men
and women dressed wholly in embroidery
and today's printed status symbols: a Coca-
Cola bottle, a Volvo badge, a key or the por-
trait of President Shagari, swinging on
bought machine-made cloth wrapped
round backsides and bosoms. This
thousand-year-old craft of blue-dyeing and
patterning is dying out. Why should a cultural heritage that has been handed down
from generation to generation since times
immemorial disappear?'

Betty began collecting vanishing patterns
of indigo-dyed materials. She now has a collection of some 500 pieces – a cultural
treasure, since local people have never been
tempted to preserve hand-made everyday

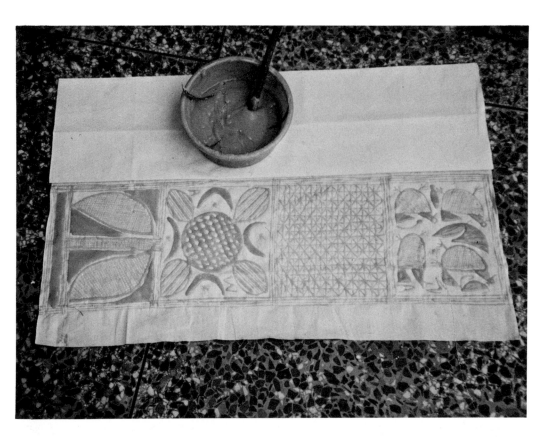

materials which have lost their status and 'gone out of their thousand-year-old fashion'. She enabled us to meet Mama Ibeji, a 50- to 60-year-old Yoruba woman whose name means 'mother of twins'. She is now a grandmother and carts a granddaughter around on her back. It is a woman's lot to look after the children, food and clothes. A grandmother has her part to play in bringing up her grandchildren. Mama Ibeji now makes her living by trading; she sells cassava roots in different markets. Ten years or so back she would instead have used the cassava to make the paste with which she used to paint the patterns on cloth. We shall see how she did it.

Mama Ibeji lights a fire on the ground and sets an enamel bowl with ground cassava, copper sulphate, alum and water over it. The quantities are approximate: a piece of alum chopped off with a machete, a cupped handful of water. She stirs it all with a piece of wood. She tells us how, when she was still so young that her breasts were mere little buds, she was apprenticed to a master-dyer for four to five years, for which privilege she had to pay her mistress and her family a high price in bananas, colanuts, palm oil, dried fish, sugar cane, salt, honey etc. The secrets of the craft and patterns used were subject to strict 'juju' and could not be taught or revealed to any Tom, Dick or Harry. The lengths of cloth were kept hidden away until they were ready. Something of the same attitude persists today, for not many of the women dyers one meets will answer questions.

The paste has now boiled for a quarter of an hour. Mama Ibeji tests it to see if it has acquired the right, tough consistency by putting a small lump of it into her mouth and chewing it like chewing gum. If ready, the paste is then strained through a piece of cloth. Next she pulls some wing-feathers from a live hen that she has caught. Now she folds a piece of material first in one direction then in the other, pressing down the folds to produce distinct lines which will guide the pattern she is to paint. Next, she spreads the cloth on the ground in front of her and, using a feather as a brush, paints a design with the ropy paste, which does not penetrate the material, but quickly dries on the surface. For a whole day she paints, squatting in different positions on the ground. By evening she has painted only a small part of the cloth which eventually will be sewn together with another of equal size to make a 'wrapper', a garment you tie round yourself like a skirt. Another half of the material has still to be painted. Then the whole is taken to the blue-dyer. Once it has acquired its blue colour and is dry, it is soaked again and the paste scraped off, revealing a white design (where the paste protected the cloth from the dye) on a blue background and plain blue on the other side. The two halves of the material are sewn together and folded, and taken to a saleswoman who sells them in the market. Each woman has to have her profit on the transaction.

Time has become money – there as here. Can people afford a creative craft? Mama Obeji cannot. She makes more money by selling cassava and oil in various markets than by practising her traditional craft. Nowadays, very little indigo cloth is sold in the markets. Where, before, people dyed their own cloth, there are now very few dyers left and no young people to take over.

Many were the questions I and my travelling companions asked ourselves in the evenings. Can a country – even our own earth – afford to allow folk textile crafts to disappear? Can one afford to protect? What is culture? What sort of world do we want? These are pertinent questions everywhere today.

Mama Ibeji painting cloth with a hen's feather. She works without a pattern and her only guides to the composition are folds in the cloth.

Pictures on pages 68–69.
Detail of painted adire-eleko:
a. zinc stencil. b. stencilled cloth from Lagos

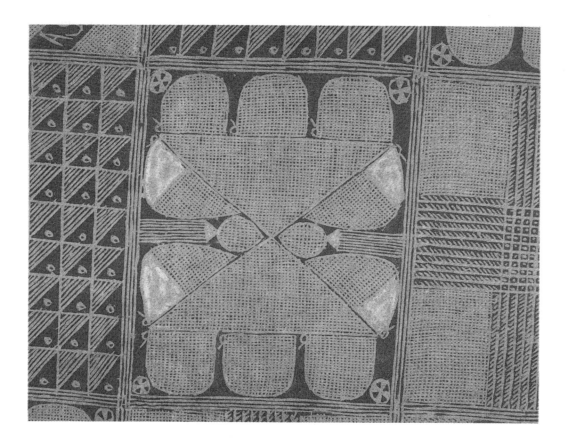

Stencilled adire-eleko

There is practically no archival documentation for the West African resist technology, so we have to rely on the oral traditions told us of the crafts and methods that still survive.

The manufacture of adire-cloth using metal stencils and pastes is thought to be no more than some hundred years old; yet there is nothing to say that it cannot be considerably older. Today's stencils are made of thin plates of zinc, previously lead, or of the tin foil used for packaging tea. The design is cut or punched out with a hollow chisel or punch in a format generally 8″ × 8″ (20 × 20 cm).

The material to be patterned is spread out and nailed down at the four corners. The stencil is put in position on the cloth and the paste is applied with a thin semi-circular metal scraper. The paste is pressed into the material and the surplus scraped off and down into a bowl beside the printer. Many designs make use of several different stencils. The design can be inscribed by drawing a comb through the paste while it is still wet. In this way parallel lines, wavy lines, circles or semi-circles can be produced. The combs used are cut with varying numbers of teeth, some small and pointed, others broad. Stencil prints tend to be slightly meagre, because of their quite simple design-surfaces. But the use of colour-screens in the larger white parts and the spontaneous effect given by scraping with a comb, can make the designs exciting.

中華人民共和國製造

Chinese and Japanese Resist-printing

Chinese blue-print

While Western dyers were still applying colours and paste to their material with wooden blocks, their Asiatic fellows were using the significantly more subtle method of stencilling. They, however, had never used the open parts of the stencil to apply the colour, as we do with our screen print templates, but instead, they applied a resist, the purpose of which was to prevent the fibres accepting the dye, in their case blue indigo. The result of this technique, used for thousands of years, the classic blue-white resist print, is characteristic of China's textile scene.

A number of sensational archaeological finds made in recent years, especially in Chiangling, Hupeh Province, and in Ch'angshe Province, have given us a tangible and quite unique insight into early Chinese dyeing technology. What has been found is a large number of dressed and woven textiles that are exceedingly well preserved and date back to the period of the Warring States (474–221 BC) and the Han period (206 BC – AD 230). Considerably earlier literary sources concerning dyeing and printing can now be checked against this material. The things found in these graves also included textiles printed in blue, red and white and produced by resist-stencilling combined with painting. There are twenty dyes that have been identified, of which those most used were blue from indigo, red from madder and yellow from gardenia. These vegetable dyes were complemented with various mineral pigments.

The high technical quality of the dyes used in these finds points to a very long tradition of experiment and to great experience in dyeing. Indigo-dyeing presupposes experience in fermentation-bath dyeing, dyeing with madder assumes familiarity with mordants and the use of pigment presupposes knowledge of suitable binding materials. We know, however, that all the different processes were specialised crafts as early as the Chou period (1122–770 BC). For example, among the many specialist departments of the Ministry for Earth was one concerned only with the collection and extraction of vegetable dyestuffs. The Ministry of Heaven had a dyeing department which dealt with questions concerning bleaching, printing and dyeing, all according to the Chinese calendar.

We know China as the land of origin of silk cultivation, but it has produced significant quantities of cotton for just as long. Many parts of the country, particularly in the East, are especially suited for this. Silk may well have become an important export early on, as well as the material used for the fine clothes of the governing class, but cotton provided the textile of everyday life, just as suitable for padding a coverlet or for stuffing their padded winter clothes, as a material for the people's blue-print.

The province of Kiangsu in Eastern China was in early times a centre of this blue-white print. Literary sources indicate that it was in common use during the Sung dynasty (AD 900–1299). From the beginning of the 15th century on, the cloth was to be found in every home in the province.

The technical and aesthetic forms reflect
(continued on page 74)

Blue-print from Kiangsu in Eastern China.
    The design is called 'Plum blossom and deer in the Spring'.

Kiangsu in Eastern China was early on a centre for producing blue-print. Sources show that this was common even during the Sung dynasty (960–1279) and from the 15th century on was to be found in almost all homes in the province.

The jacket of the Chinese rice-farmer has been coloured with indigo since time immemorial. The reason for this is said to be that cloth dyed with indigo is many times stronger than undyed cloth and that it keeps insects and snakes at a distance, which is a considerable advantage for those working in open fields.

Contemporary Chinese blue-print sold by the yard. This is manufactured today using more or less the same old method. The material used is home-woven cotton, and this means that the width cannot exceed 16″ (40 cm). The resist-paste is made of soya beans and lime, the dye is genuine indigo

how deeply rooted they were in the people. The design of the patterns and the cutting of the stencils and the actual dyeing have long been carried out by rural craftsmen, a fact which explains their very characteristic appearance, often reminiscent of the simple, energetic lines of the paper-cutter. Their motifs reflect the images of everyday country living and people's hopes for a long and happy existence. The roe deer is a symbol of long life, the chrysanthemum symbolises courage, since it flowers in the cold weather and orchids are symbols of personal integrity.

Japanese stencil-print, Kata-zome

Japanese resist-printed cloths have long been famous for conveying a powerful, sometimes almost dramatic message. Their form of expression has been refined by using craftsmanship and aesthetic sense to perfect the technical possibilities to a degree that is difficult to comprehend. With just a simple paste, paper patterns and a single colour – indigo-blue – the Japanese have produced cloth of unusual beauty.

The Japanese name for their method is *kata-zome*. The term comes from the word *kata* meaning a tool which can be used to repeat a pattern or a shape etc. and *zome* from the verb *someru*, to dye. The resist-paste is made of a steamed mixture of rice-flour and husks, lime and salt, as mentioned previously. Its production, however, is not an exact science, its quality being decided more by eye, feel and experience, than by following exactly prescribed quantities and instructions. Its main ingredients are finely ground flour from a special kind of glutinous rice, mochi-rice, which has an exceptional adhesive quality, so that it attaches itself strongly to the material. The husk, *komonnuka*, acts as a filling and counteracts the rice's extreme stickiness, making it easier to wash the paste away.

Paper-stencil, Kata-gami, from the mid-19th century with a design of chrysanthemums. The area reproduced measures 15″ × 15″ (37.5 × 37.5 cm).

Top, left.
Detail of an old Japanese stencil-print using the famous 'sacred crane' motif.

Lime makes the paste denser and at the same time acts as a preservative, while the salt functions as a hygroscopic substance and so prevents excessive drying of the paste. The quantity of salt is adjusted according to prevailing conditions and the amount of moisture in the atmosphere. In very dry weather, the amount of salt may have to be doubled or even trebled.

The stencils, *kata-gami*, through which the paste is applied to the material, are made of stout, hand-made paper prepared from the bark of the kozo, the paper-mulberry tree. From two to four layers of paper are stuck together with the sticky juice of unripe persimmons. After this lamination process the paper is dried in the sun and then hung up in a smoke-filled room for some ten days. The combination of tanning-agent in the persimmon juice and resin from the smoke makes the paper stout and waterproof.

The method of perforating the stencil with the required design has not changed significantly in the last several centuries. Six to twenty sheets of this special paper are placed in a pile and fastened down so that they cannot slide out of place while the work is being performed. Once the pile of sheets is placed on a table of some hard, dense timber, the perforation is done using specially shaped knives and punches, which cut through all the sheets. Finally, each stencil is strengthened by placing silk-gauze over the whole surface.

The cloth to be patterned is laid out on a long table, the stencil is placed in the required position and the paste applied through it using a thin wooden scraper with a handle. When the paste has dried the cloth is stretched by inserting narrow, pointed bamboo rods from selvage to selvage on the reverse side at each end.

The dyeing (with indigo), *ai-zome*, is carried out by and large in the same way as has been described when telling of its use in other places; i.e. the cloth is immersed in cement tanks or vats sunk into the ground. In Japan these are normally arranged in groups of four with an arrangement for heating in the middle of each group. The bath used was often a zinc-lime bath or a fermentation-bath.

The production of the actual indigo-dye was, briefly, that the leaves (of *Polygonum tinctorium*), with the more woody parts removed, were packed together on the floor of a special building, moistened and covered with an insulating layer. After this vegetable mass had fermented for 80–90 days, during which time it was moistened again at intervals, blackish lumps of indigo had formed (*sukomi-ai*), and these were then crushed in a mortar and made into a paste, which was then shaped into indigo balls for delivery to the indigo-dyers.

During the Tenna period, towards the end of the 17th century, there was an artist, called Yuzensai Miyasaki, whose principal occupation was the preparation of designs for kimonos. His search for new procedures led to the discovery that if you added powdered mussel shell to the ordinary rice-paste, this produced a much better paste for white-resist. This led to further refinement, at the end of which by using a copper nozzle fitted to a paper forcing-bag (*kappa*), he was able to draw continuous resist lines of extreme delicacy. Continued experimentation led to his being able to apply coloured dyes within the white outlines of the pattern. This new method allowed considerable freedom and spontaneity and brought the artist great renown.

Japanese coloured woodcut. The garment is decorated with the family emblem, a gentian flower, made by using resist-paste.

A forcing-bag (in Japanese *kappa*) made of rice-paper with a copper nozzle with which a resist-design can be applied free-hand to the material.

Detail of Japanese resist-painting, made with a *kappa* in Kyoto, probably during the latter half of the 19th century.

WAX BATIK

A fabric decorated with batik technique is produced by the alternate application of resist-wax and dyes. The procedure differs from blue-print above all in that the resist – beeswax and resin – is considerably more pliant and much better able to resist than pastes made of flour or clay, thus making freer and more spontaneous designs possible, as well as enriching the choice of colours. This technique has come to be associated above all with Indonesian textile work. For centuries the production of batik, particularly in Java, has been perfected and refined to produce a product that is unique and a national treasure.

Batik of the Meo

The production of batik is important in another textile-culture, though there it is different both in formation and use. This culture is that of the Meo people of northern Thailand, who live in almost inaccessible mountain villages and who are the only people on the mainland of South-east Asia who use the technique.

This area is often called the Golden Triangle and is inhabited by groups of people who once migrated there from south-eastern and south-central China. The group consists of two main branches: Hmong Deaw (White Meo) and Mong Njua (literally green Meo, but usually called the Blue Meo).

The old Meo legends recount how their ancestors once lived in an icy land, where the winters were hard and the nights long. This has led to speculation that they came to China from Tibet, Siberia or Mongolia. Need of freedom and independence have forced the Meo to move on every now and again in their search for areas where these needs could be met. During the Second World War, the Chinese nationalist government tried to forbid the Meo using their own tongue or wearing their special dress, but this merely enhanced their self-esteem and strengthened their need to be independent, with the result that fresh groups of the Meo left China.

The batik-patterned products made by the women of the Blue Meo are used only for their strongly pleated skirts and their 'baby-carriers'. The skirt calls for about 23' (7 m) of cloth 1' (30 cm) wide. Although cotton is the easiest material to obtain, the Meo women prefer hemp because of its weight and gloss. They start by dividing the cloth

into rectangles, which are marked out with a pointed piece of metal, like an old aluminium spoon. The wax, from the village's own hives, is applied with an applicator made of sheet-copper with a slim bamboo handle. In shape it resembles a flattened cornet with a narrow opening in the bottom. To make one of these that will function properly is so difficult that there is not a smith in every village capable of producing one.

The wax is applied in short, straight lines. No curves or soft lines are allowed and the only element, other than straight lines, used in a Meo design is dots or groups of dots and little crosses. The difference between Javanese batik and that of the Meo is striking, and is to be explained by differences in textile material and in the design of the applicator. The Javanese version of this latter has a fine discharge tube which permits very free drawing with the wax on the surface of the cloth, while the closely woven, smooth cotton fabric in its turn makes very fine, almost graceful ornamentation possible. The hempen cloth used by the Meo women with its coarser texture, plus the different design of the applicator, give their product a special and quite different character.

To be able to make the batik-patterned part of the Meo skirt is considered a personal achievement and assures one of considerable standing among the women of the village. Usually only two or three in each village are considered sufficiently skilled. Young Meo girls start learning to draw the

The drawing above is of a Meo applicator from Chiang-Mai.

Baby-carrier used by the Meo of Hmong. The larger blue-white area is patterned with batik; the lesser area has an embroidered centre.

The photograph on the right shows a baby-carrier in use.

Waxed cloths from Chiang-Mai, one indigo-dyed, one boiled.

designs when they are five or ten, though they may not necessarily become skilled enough to do so later.

When the long length of cloth has been properly waxed, dyed with indigo and 'cooked', small red ribbons are sewn onto certain parts of the blue-white surface, before this is joined up with the other parts of the skirt. It can take between six months and a year to make a skirt and to own more than one is a sign almost of extravagance. Not even the richest women have more than a few.

The skirt's pleats are made permanent by dipping the skirt into rice-starch and then pressing the pleats between two flat stones. A stout thread goes through all the folds and this is used to draw the whole skirt together when it is not being used.

A Meo bride leaves her parental home on her wedding day, but before this she will have displayed her whole trousseau and what she is taking to her new home. Here, a batik-patterned, pleated skirt is one of the attractions.

As well as for skirts, batik is used for the middle of the 'baby-carrier', and for this the central blue-white design is surrounded with highly coloured ribbons, making the size of the whole some $18'' \times 22''$ $(45 \times 55$ cm$)$. A smaller rectangle of some $6'' \times 10''$ $(15 \times 25$ cm$)$ with an embroidered centre is fastened to the upper part, after which two long ribbons are attached, one to either side, so that the mother can tie her child on securely.

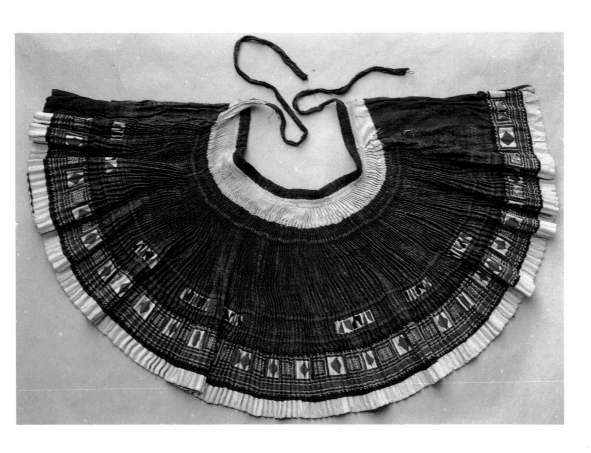

Meo skirt from Chiang-Rai in Northern Thailand. The patterning is wax-batik, appliqué work and embroidery.

Preparation of indigo and dyeing

The indigo plant, *Indigofera tinctoria*, buds roughly at the season of the first rains, that is late in April, and is reckoned to yield two harvests, one in June and another at the end of October. When cut, the plant is about 2′ (60 cm) high. The plants are gathered and laid in wooden troughs filled with water and left there for several days. On the second day, the whole mass is turned so as to ensure that it is soaked through and through. Lime is added to the fermenting contents of each trough, which now has a very strong smell. As soon as the dye-stuff has formed, the dye-bath is prepared with water, alkaline lye and lime. A glass of strong rice-whisky is then added and the bath allowed to stand undisturbed for several days. After the fourth day blue bubbles will appear on the surface of the liquor, showing that the indigo has begun to dissolve. When the bubbles are coming strongly and no longer burst easily, this will mean that the bath is ready for use; otherwise more rice-whisky has to be added. Once the bath is ready, the cloth is lowered into it and worked for about half an hour. It is then hung up on a wooden frame protected from sunlight, so that the dye can oxidise out. Further working in the bath and subsequent oxidisation continue until the desired deep-blue colour has been achieved.

One drop of indigo is enough to spoil a whole bowl of milk –
Javanese proverb

Javanese Batik

It would not be incorrect to say that the high quality of Javanese batik is the result of an exceptionally good set of local circumstances, i.e. access to dye-stuffs, textile material and tools, but it is not the whole truth. The Indian national epic, *Ramayana*, records how one of the characters was instructed thus: 'Thoroughly investigate Yawadwipa (Java) renowned for its seven kingdoms, island of gold and silver.' Java was a concept familiar to the Greek geographer Ptolemy, as it was to the Chinese traveller Fa-Hian. These and other early sources give the impression that the people of Java were highly cultured even early in the Christian era, and it is perhaps against this background that we should look for the truth as to why their form of resist-patterning achieved such a degree of aesthetic perfection.

The production of batik is as much an expression of Javanese culture as are its music, dances and Wayang theatre. Their textile works of art produced by the batik technique are not, however, intended to be seen at rest and two-dimensionally. Batik-patterned cloth is intended to be worn, to be an article of dress both for everyday and for festive occasions. When it covers the soft and graceful movements of dancers, or when, to the rhythmic accompaniment of a gamelan orchestra it is draped round the bride as she approaches the groom, then it is that the symbols emerge, the ornaments come to life and the surface of the material glows.

No one knows what the word 'batik' means. It, perhaps, derives from the Malay word *tik* which means 'drop', or point, and then via *ambatik*, meaning line of dots, drawing, acquired its present form and meaning. When and, especially, from where batik came to Java is another subject of considerable, but vague, speculation. Some people think that it came, via the Singhalese, from East India; others again maintain that it is peculiar to Indonesia, an original art form. A very primitive form of it has been encountered on the island of Flores, east of Java.

The basic material for batik work has always been almost exclusively cotton. Silk is sometimes used, but only in coastal areas where Chinese influence has been particularly strong. Down the ages, princely ceremonial garments and popular clothes have always been made of what we sometimes consider a rather simple material, cotton. There are several reasons for this: one is the demands put on the fabric by the different processes to which it is subjected: dyeing, boiling etc. Then there is the aesthetic requirement that the detailed design of batik calls for a material that will allow it to come into its own, and fine, closely woven cotton of high quality is the only material that meets all these requirements.

Batik work from Central Java dyed with indigo and soga. These three illustrate the superiority of indigo as a dye. The top illustration is of batik made in the 1940s which has never been used; the middle example is from the early 20th century and its brown portions have faded badly. The bottom specimen is from the 19th century and here the brown soga-colour has faded completely, while the indigo is to all intents and purposes unaltered.

Applicators from Bandung, West Java. One has a coarse discharge pipe for drawing broad lines and whole surfaces; the other has two narrow nozzles for drawing parallel lines.

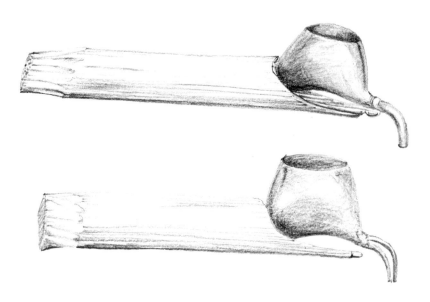

The special tool for applying the wax, *tjanting*, as used in Java, consists of a small reservoir made of thin copper sheet and fitted with one or more discharge pipes, with a handle of some light wood. The discharge pipe can be so narrow that you can draw more or less hair-fine lines of wax or rows of dots on the cloth.

The West early realised that its colonies and other distant areas were valuable suppliers of cheap raw materials. Nor was it long before it was realised that the traffic in goods could go both ways, that the West's distant possessions offered a potential market for the products of the West's growing industries. Where Indonesia was concerned, this meant that even as early as the first half of the 19th century quantities of European machine-printed imitations of the old batik designs were imported into Java and other East Indian islands. Competition was so ruthless, that, at the turn of the century, people were prophesying the early demise

of batik art. But this did not happen. Instead, the Javanese developed a new form altogether of the age-old technique, stamp-batik (*batik tjap*). Here whole areas of a design or larger connected parts of an ornament were transferred to the cotton fabric with a copper stamp that had been dipped in a wax mixture. This so successfully rationalised production, and made it cheaper, that it saved batik. After Indonesia acquired independence at the end of the Second World War, laws were passed that protected the country's assets, of which batik is one.

The colour scale of classic Javanese batik is strict and very limited. The main, and until the 17th century, the only colours were blue and white. During the 17th century this was extended by the addition of brown and soon after that, having acquired knowledge of mordant metal salts, yellow and red were added as well. One of Linnaeus' pupils, Carl Peter Thunberg, writing of his visit to the East Indian archipelago in the 1770s,

tells how the indigo bush (*Indigofera anil*) grew wild all over Java and how it was generally used to produce their blue dye-stuff. He mentions, too, that indigo was one of the goods, along with rice, spices and calico, that were exported from the islands at the time when he was there.

Though women always make the hand-drawn designs when using a tjanting, it is men who perform the simpler task of producing stamp-batik. It is the men, too, who do all the dyeing. Early descriptions of a Javanese blue-dyer's workshop tell how there could be up to fifty large earthenware jars there, in which he prepared the indigo-bath and carried out the actual dyeing. The dye-works that I myself have been able to visit used other and considerably more rational procedures for dyeing with indigo. The pieces of cloth were lowered into deep troughs, the top edges of which were level with the ground. Batik work up to 10′ (3 m) long could be hung straight down into the

High Javanese batik, detail of a Garuda motif.

bath and there would still be a free space underneath where sediment could accumulate. A stout frame to which the pieces of cloth were fastened was raised by a special apparatus clear of the bath, after which the individual pieces of cloth were separated, using long rods, so that oxidisation could be as complete as possible. As soon as one set of pieces had been lifted out, another was automatically lowered in. It called for twenty or so dippings of about five minutes each and as many oxidisations to achieve a saturated dark shade of indigo. Strong boiling and rinsing to remove the wax and excess dye completed the process.

87

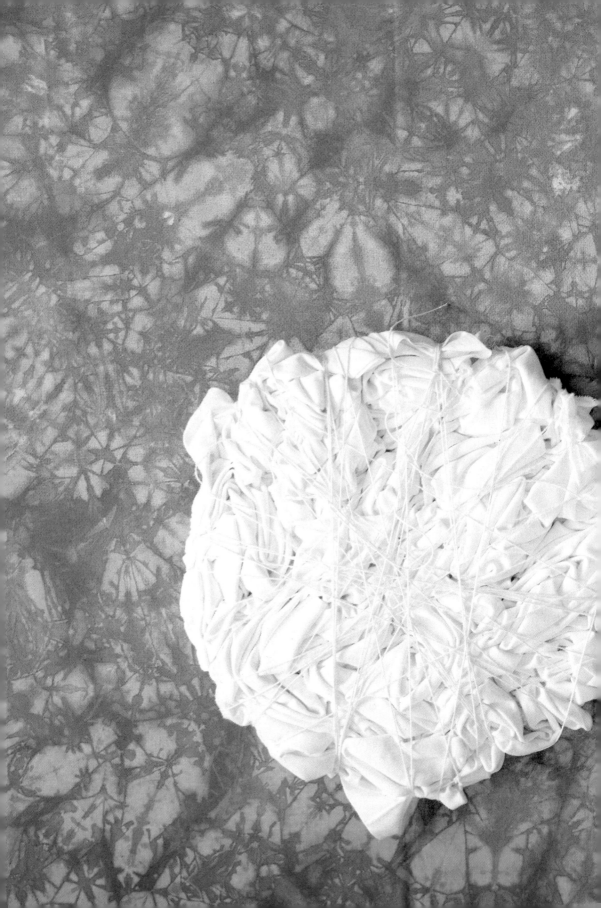

PLANGI – TIE-DYEING

The resist-technique that goes under the name *plangi*, or tie-dyeing, is often very striking in its designs, but technically less demanding than paste-, wax- or ikat-products. It comprises a number of methods, all of which involve deliberate pulling together, or up, of the material and tying it, before the actual dyeing. The plangi technique has been practised by different peoples in many parts of the world, but we still do not know when and where it originated. The earliest mentions of it are from India and Java and go back to the sixth and seventh centuries, while Chinese silk plangi has been discovered in graves along the old Silk Road. Fragments of tie-batik have also been found in Inca graves in Peru.

Plangi (tie-dyeing) from Gambia in West Africa. The pattern is a form of 'marbling' and is produced by systematically pulling the material up into a ball which is fixed by winding a stout thread round it before dyeing.

Detail of plangi (tie-dyeing) from Nigeria, West Africa.

The pattern has been produced by tieing in small seeds (some 35,000 of them!) before the cloth is dyed with indigo. The design is called 'Assembly' or 'The Emir and his people'. Total area 7′ × 12′ (210 × 360 cm).

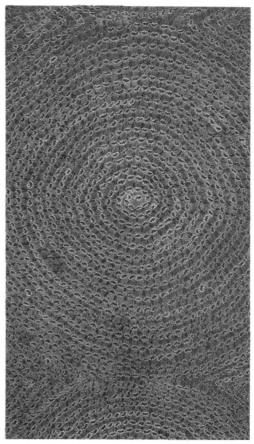

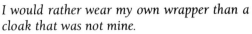

I would rather wear my own wrapper than a cloak that was not mine.

African proverb

West African Plangi

The Yoruba people of West Africa have developed a number of interesting variants of the plangi technique, ranging from the very simple and original, so-called pure plangi, which just consists of small bits of the material being drawn up and tied, to complicated patterns achieved with needle and thread and inserted into larger main shapes. Whatever the method of production, they are all known as *adire* fabrics. The word adire literally means 'tie and dye'. The basic material is always cotton and the dye almost without exception indigo, sometimes in combination with the brown *kola* dye. The thread used to tie the various folds and which sometimes has to act as a resist, is made of fibres from the leaves of the Raffia palm. Cotton threads of different thicknesses are also occasionally used. Often, some threads are left in a finished piece so as to provide the buyer with a guarantee that the material is newly made and handmade; very much the same thing is done in India, where plangi (*bandhana*) is sold still more or less tied. Adire is traditionally two lengths of 7′ (2.25 m) long and 3′ (1 m) wide put together to make what to all intents and purposes is a square of the size required for a *lappa*. These cloths used to be wrapped round the body and kept in place by twisting the upper end into the other.

African adire, which never aspires to perfection, has a vitality and imaginativeness and radiance that few fabrics, in my opinion, can match. To me it makes a congenial synthesis of the country and its people.

Adire fabrics, cut up and sewn together into fashionable garments, are a contradiction of its ethical and aesthetic values.

Forms of pattern

One of the simplest and yet most well-liked forms of pattern is produced by systematically 'plucking up' the cloth until it is gathered in a ball or thick slab which is then fixed by a thin network of thread. After dyeing you get a piece of cloth that appears to have been marbled.

Another, and probably an original method, is to draw up larger or smaller parts of the surface area, which are then tied. The size of the tied pieces can vary from those of a few millimetres to some that cover almost the whole cloth.

Then there is *adire-alabere*, the name given to the form where a thread is used to draw together parts, lines or surfaces of the cloth. The stitch can be ordinary tacking-stitch that follows a pattern that has been drawn on the material or the thread is drawn through folded parts, which are then pulled up tight.

There are no real problems involved in dyeing adire fabrics with indigo. It is done in the way described in the section on *adire-eleko*.

Chinese and Japanese Plangi

Short winter kimono (*Haori*) from Aomori prefecture in northern Japan. It is made of twin layers of cloth of which the outer is patterned in ikat (*kasuri*) and plangi (*shibori*) techniques. Probably made in the early 1900s.

Japanese kimono material in plangi, called *tatsu-maki arashi*. The fabric was made in Arimatsu by Reiichi Suzuki and his wife, who, today, are the only ones capable of making this extremely intricate form of plangi.

Chinese plangi – Jiao-xie

Along the Silk Road, the great trade route that once long ago linked East Asia with the West, lay a number of important staging posts. In the ruins of one of these old oases, Astana, archaeological excavations carried out in 1967 uncovered, amongst other things, fragments of cloth that had been patterned in plangi technique. Some years

previously, in a grave in western Liang, dated AD 418, a fragment of similar material (unbleached silk) with the same ornamentation had also been found. This is considered to be the oldest known example of Chinese plangi yet to be discovered. The actual pattern consists of resist rectangles of $\frac{1}{4}''$ (5 mm) with a dot in the middle, this being repeated in rows over the whole surface of the cloth.

In another grave at the same place, dated AD 683, they found a fragment of thin silk gauze, which is of special interest, in that the surface is covered with rhomboid pattern-elements produced by using a strong thread to draw together folded layers of the material before dyeing. Holes left by the needle and thread are clearly visible on the resist surfaces. This is, thus, a very early version of the form of plangi usually called *tritik*. In Astana they also found a number of colourful painted wooden grave figurines of the Tang dynasty (AD 618–907), some of which still had on them parts of their original dress made of real cloth; for example, two of them had shawls draped round their shoulders and these were resist-dyed in a pattern of small open rings arranged in groups of three and three.

Japanese plangi – Shibori (Yuhata)

Usually, there are considerable difficulties in the dating of the genesis and early spread of a technique within a certain area, and here Japanese plangi technique is no exception.

The oldest plangi-patterned cloth preserved in Japan is from the eighth century and thus several centuries younger than its Chinese counterparts. Nor is it, as far as can be judged, of Japanese origin, but probably imported from China, with which country Japan had active links as early as the sixth century. Naturally, this does not mean that the Japanese had not mastered the tech-

nique as such much earlier. In her book, *Tsujigahana*, Toshiko Ito maintains that the use of resist technique in Japan could go back to prehistoric times, and that the Japanese then knew of methods of tying up cloth in such a way that certain parts of it were protected from the dye.

The word presently used for all forms of plangi is *shibori*, but the original, native word was *yuhata* (*yu* = tie, *hata* = cloth) and this would seem to indicate that the plangi technique was known before the introduction of Buddhism and the art of writing which reached the Japanese islands in the sixth century. There is considerable literary evidence of the use of plangi materials and its gradually widespread use throughout the country. In the *Japanese Chronicle* (*Nihon Shoki*) published in AD 720 there is mention of rolls of resist-dyed silk being among the gifts presented to foreign ambassadors. This is a clear indication that at that time plangi technique must have been at a high level, both technically and artistically.

Another example of the value attached to plangi materials is to be found in *Engi shiki* (a 50 volume history) which is an important source of information about tenth-century Japan. There we are told how you could pay your taxes by delivering plangi-patterned silk materials, a system not unlike our own earlier one, when you could pay church or state dues *in natura*.

During the 11th and 12th centuries, plangi-patterned clothes were worn by all classes of society and used as well for a number of other purposes. A document bearing the date 1088 tells how a noble from Fujiwara sailed his ship under a plangi-patterned banner. Another noble, a member of the Taira clan, wrote in his diary for 1154 of Buddhist ceremonies and imperial festivities in which plangi played a large part. One description of the imperial palace tells how the large surfaces indoors were divided up with draperies executed in plangi, and how at an imperial banquet the courtiers and their wives were all dressed in plangi-ornamented garments. Even the women

who cooked and served the food wore skirts and aprons of small-patterned plangi.

Towards the end of the 12th century Japanese artists had developed their own distinct style of painting, depicting with accurate observation and considerable humour Japanese subjects and phenomena. In even the earliest of these paintings the clothes of the persons depicted and their patterns are an important element. Here, we encounter the plangi motif, in Japan called *kumo-shibori* (gossamer plangi) which is produced by drawing up a part of the fabric and tying it lightly with a waxed thread that holds it in place until it has been dyed.

In the work of the great Japanese masters of the wood-cut of the 17th and 18th centuries, Masanobu, Utamaro, Toyokuni and many others, one can follow the development of, and the changes in, patterns used in Japanese dress in a clear and understandable way. Their realism and the wealth of detail are important for any study of them.

Detail of plangi-patterned fabric from Southern China. The pattern is achieved by tying small seeds into the cloth before dyeing with indigo.

In the parts of the world where plangi-patterning is used, production is most often restricted to a few variants of the basic forms: marbling, folding, *tritik* etc. In Japan, however, a number of new and effective variants have been developed. One of these (*kanoko*) employs extremely small, regularly spaced ridges which fill up the surfaces and provide ornamental detail which is yet the whole time subordinated to a master pattern. Contrast is provided by the large, powerful, dominant ridges, whose language is enhanced by colour contrasts. The deep-blue of indigo is more suited to this than any

The dye-shop of a Japanese plangi-master. The dyeing tanks are a couple of metres deep and are arranged in groups of four with a heating apparatus in the middle. The ready-tied fabric is lowered flat into the bath and kept extended with the help of thin bamboo rods with metal pins at either end. The lower part of each length of cloth is protected from sediment on the bottom of the tank by baskets placed curved side up. These baskets have the same function as the European blue-dyer's 'bath-ring'.

other colour. But dyers usually made use of some of the folding methods of plangi, in which wooden plates were used to keep the cloth pressed together during dyeing. This process is called *ita-jime* (*ita* = a wooden plate, *jime* = to press together), a word that is also used for the ikat-form, where a course of thread is reserved by compressing it between plates.

Small-scale plangi with diminutive circles and rectangles can be produced in different ways. In the first place by gathering up the material bit by bit into conical shapes which are then 'fixed' with thread or other material. Special tools have been designed that simplify their work. Another way is to employ a wooden block with vertical wooden pegs against which the material is pressed firmly and the resulting 'tops' of the material are then fixed with waxed thread. The use of such plates with pegs arranged in a complete design (*kata*) constitutes a considerable simplification of richly

decorated forms of plangi. Small pieces of protruding cloth can be shaped into squares quite easily if the material is two-leaved twill, relatively thin and elastic and is drawn or pressed (against a wooden peg) before being fixed with thread, bamboo-ring or something of the kind.

This renaissance in Japanese textile crafts and the personal re-interpretation of old techniques in recent years has given a much-needed, vitalising stimulus to our often set and limited designs.

Hiroyokoh Shindoh of Kyoto, shown here, prefers the traditional fermentation-bath with its lime and nutrients for micro-organisms to the modern hydrogen sulphite bath. He considers that in this way he achieves improved resistance to wet and rubbing in the finished product. The fabrics he uses come from China and are carefully washed in lye before they are tied and dyed. As resist he will also use bits of cloth that are sewn on.

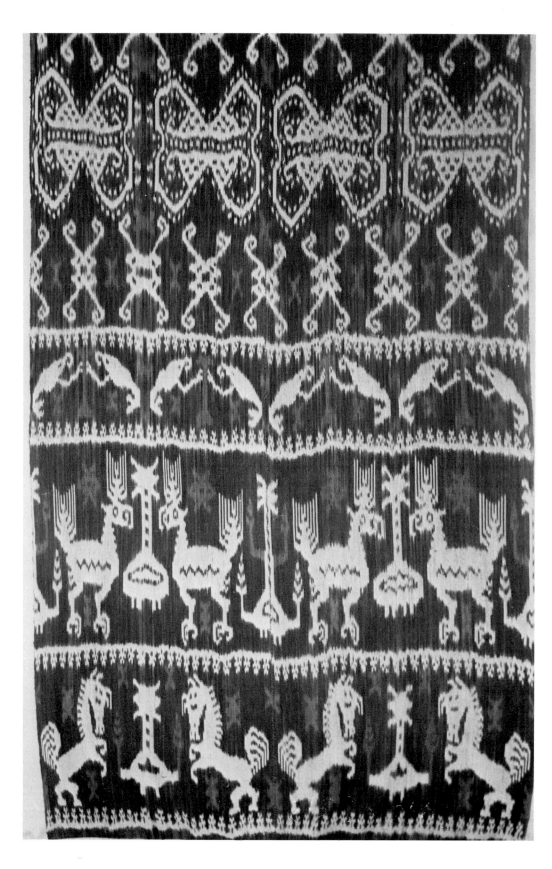

IKAT

Most resist techniques are used to pattern fabrics that have already been dyed. The ikat process on the other hand applies the resist protective layers to the yarns with which a fabric will later be produced. The term ikat comes from the Malay-Indonesian word *meng-ikat* which means tie, twine, knot and has long been used in the original and true meaning, that of a comprehensive term for fabric patterned by some method of yarn-resist. However, today the concept ikat has acquired a considerably wider significance and now includes a number of ikat-related techniques, which are not necessarily based on tying-processes, but whose result has a distinct ikat-like appearance. Thus today, the term ikat is used more for the visual appearance of the finished textile than to describe the techniques used to achieve it.

Indonesian Ikat

East Asia is one of several possible centres where the ikat-technique may have originated. Indonesia has occupied a special position here and in that huge archipelago all forms of ikat have been produced and in many places are still produced in significant quantities. The predominant colours used in this ikat are blue, red and white, sometimes with sparing use of yellow and black as well.

The blue dye is produced in the same way and using the same basic ingredients as we have seen used in other cultures, i.e. indigo, lime and lye. As well as these basic substances each dyer adds his own special ones. Many will not reveal their methods, because often it is not just a question of special substances, but also of magical ritual thought

to be important for a successful result. In some places you find that the magical element is considered as significant as the purely practical work of preparing the ikat-yarn and even the dye-bath. One idea often encountered in Indonesia and elsewhere in connection with the dyeing process is that women who are menstruating or are pregnant should not be allowed even near the dye-bath, as their presence would spoil the result. However, the boundary between superstition and practical observation is, to say the least of it, vague. Another old idea is that citrus fruit should not be picked close to a dye-bath under reduction; another, that feathered fowl must not come near the bath. There is a practical element here, since an indigo-bath is extremely pH sensitive and citric acid, like uric acid in bird's urine and droppings, could upset the alkaline balance of the bath.

On Sumba and Savu, where the women who weave the ikat also attend to its dyeing, the area in which indigo is handled is fenced off and men are not allowed inside in case their presence might prejudice the result.

Here indigo is scarce and the dye-stuff is

Man's cloak (*hinggi*) from Eastern Sumba, Indonesia.
Warp-ikat in cotton, about 3′ × 8′ (83 × 230 cm), in two shades of indigo-blue and white. The design is characteristic of Sumba ikat, which assembles the figures and decorative elements in wide horizontal fields.

Cloak (*sibolang*) from Toba-Batak district in Northern Sumatra. Warp-ikat in cotton, 38″ × 98½″ (96 × 246 cm). The fabric is finished with a narrow hem of red, black and white woven into it. A sibolang often constitutes a highly valued gift, usually a wedding present.

Sarong from the island of Savu, Indonesia.

Warp-ikat in cotton sewn up to make a sarong 22″ × 58″ (55 × 145 cm) (total area 44″ × 58″ or 110 × 145 cm). The design is characteristic of Savu women's dress. The broad ikat-patterned fields are balanced by narrower plain or patterned edges. The colours are deep indigo-blue, 'Turkey red', from *Morinda citrifolia*, and white, that is to say, undyed.

obtained by a process that differs from the usual. The indigo leaves are collected and allowed to ferment in water to which lime has been added, the whole being stirred all the while. The leaves are then strained through a tightly woven basket, a procedure that deposits a scum of pigmented indigo on the sides. Indigo obtained in this way is very pure and of high quality. It is collected, dried and then used to prepare the dye-bath together with water and lye. A number of dyers are not particular as to the species of tree from which the lye is prepared; indeed, some are content with ordinary ash from the hearth. Other dyers are very particular and will use only ash from one particular kind of wood or bark from another. Most prepare a lye that is then poured into the bath, but in Savu the ash is put straight into the dye-bath.

The finished cloth is washed in sea-water which improves the fastness. On the island of Rote it is laid on salt sea-sand for the same purpose.

Japanese Ikat – Kasuri

No country has developed more variants in ikat technique than Japan. Here, the traditional methods have been augmented with a number of unique procedures for a more rational and direct patterning of the yarn: for example, by painting and printing on the warp, partial dyeing without resist, plus the *ita-jime* method, where the resist is applied to the yarn by compressing it between patterned wooden plates.

The usual term applied to all forms is *kasuri*, phonetically associated with a number of words relating to the subtly diffuse character of ikat, such as *kasumi* which means mist or fog.

Specimens of ikat from the Anuka and Nara periods (AD 593–710) have been found, showing that the technique was early in use there. However, the general and many-sided use, which is so evident today, came about just when the cotton-plant was introduced some 200 years ago. Before that they had used rami, hemp and banana fibre, materials that are difficult to dye.

Detail of a twin ikat-patterned fabric from Kyoto, Japan.

The design has been achieved by resist-dyeing both the warp- and the weft-threads. The material, probably made in the early 20th century, has been used to make a padded winter kimono. Its dark-blue colour has been achieved by treating the yarn with clay or mud containing iron during the dyeing process.

A printed *ajrak* from Sind, Pakistan.

Printed calicos from the Indian sub-continent have taken many different forms. Different techniques of production have found varying aesthetic expression. Th. Salmon wrote in 1731 that 'the people of the Coromandel Coast paint their calicos with a brush; but those living in the North print them', i.e. with blocks. Irrespective of the printing method used they all have one thing in common: the basic material is always cotton, often of high quality, and the dyes, as a rule, are indigo and madder, the patterning-technique is a combination of resist- and mordant procedures.

In the province of Sind in the Indus Valley they manufacture a cloth called *ajrak* using age-old methods. The name, which appears to be an old Arabic word meaning 'blue', suggests that the cloth originated in days gone-by when the province's cloth was printed with simple clay- (or clay-and-resin) resist and indigo and thus was confined to blue with white decoration. Today's ajrak, as the pictures above and to the right show, uses blue-black, red and white.

'Here they produce the finest and loveliest cotton fabrics in the world'.
Marco Polo writing of the kingdom of Malabar on the west coast of India.

INDIGO – TURKEY RED

For a considerable period of time and in many parts of the world textiles have been dyed with indigo alone or in combination with the natural colours of different fibres; in the first place white, but also grey, brown and black. For this, indigo has been used by many peoples and in many connections right up to our day, as is borne out by West African adire-fabrics, the Tuaregs' garments and the blue print from China and Japan, to mention but a few. All this shows not only that indigo was the only substantive dye possessing really good fastness, but that it was the only dye that could satisfactorily articulate a textile design without the assistance of other colours. It has a colour range from the most subtle light-blue to the darkest blue-black.

It took a long time for a colour with a fastness to rubbing which was also good enough to compete with the blue shades of indigo to appear on the scene. Gradually it became possible to obtain a red dye-stuff from the roots of different species of Rubia and members of the Rubia family; and also to develop a method using mordants that made it possible to apply the dye to vegetable material. For some thousands of years red dye and deep-blue indigo formed a constellation which we have come to regard as classic.

Indian Resist-printing

It is not clear how this red dye and the technique of applying it to textile fibres developed. Finds made during excavations at Mohenjo-Daro in the Indus valley show that the Indian craft of dyeing goes back as far as the second and third millennia BC. The textiles found in the excavations there include fragments of cotton materials that have been mordanted and dyed with a dye from some species of madder. Perhaps here we shall find the beginning of what much later was to be the famous and attractive fabrics of which Marco Polo and other early travellers in Asia wrote so ecstatically and whose imaginative designs and strong colours were to sweep Europe centuries later. The Fustat finds earlier mentioned, finds of blue-white-red Indian resist-printing, must however not be regarded as representing the acme of craftsmanship of the Indian dyers. It is probable that they should rather be regarded as relatively cheap export goods made for the Egyptian market, though we, seeing them so much later in time, find them both interesting and attractive.

The printed cloth of medieval Europe was produced by using simple carved wooden blocks by means of which a black or black and red oil-based pigment was transferred to the cloth. The result must be regarded more as a form of painting than of dyeing. The textile material felt less and less like cloth and, obviously, there could be no question of washing other than as a very light procedure.

For centuries the West had heard of Indian printed fabrics from Hyderabad, Ahmedabad or the Coromandel coast, bizarre and as inaccessible as the Orient's spices, gold and precious stones. But no sooner had traffic been established for good and all by the ships of the East India companies in the 17th and 18th centuries than the situation quickly changed. Now, at last, it became possible for members of the European public to acquire those multi-coloured materials. The encounter was both dramatic and a shock. Indian calicos, as they were sometimes called, were in many respects the opposite of the European prints. They had graceful, perfectly fashioned designs and strong, clear colours. The fabric was dyed through and through allowing the delicate cotton to come into its own. Lastly, they also had the great advantage that these fabrics could be washed without harming the colour.

It should, perhaps, be emphasised that to call the Indian calicos 'prints' is very misleading, since the colours were mostly applied by dipping the cloth and treating it in a proper dye-bath. As transpires from the following, it is really a question of a combined process, the major part of which is a resist- or mordant-process. How, later, the resist or mordant substances were applied to the base-material is of secondary impor-

tance. There are many different ways of doing it: painting, print etc.

Not many works of any comprehensiveness have been written on Indian textile printing and its methods, and this is not surprising. The procedure is extremely complicated and Indian dyers carried out the different procedures only from their own experiences and ability and without any instruction handbooks to guide them. There was no uniform procedure, this varied from craftsman to craftsman and from place to place. However, it is possible to reconstruct the main procedures from the accounts of the German scientist S. Hermbstedt (1811) and Th. Salmon's description of the Coromandel coast of 1721. Production begins with 'inner preparation' which involved some 50 per cent bleaching of the cloth. Then came repeated treatment in a watery emulsion of some fatty substance (usually buffalo milk) which also contained a tanning agent. Preparation concluded with the material being wrung out and dried in the sun for a day or so, after which it was washed and once again dried.

The 'outer preparation' began by the cloth being pounded with a wooden club against a hard underlay to make the surface as smooth and even as possible before the next stage, in which the design was transferred to the cloth with the help of a perforated paper template and pulverised charcoal in a little cloth bag. This gave the outline which was then filled in with a feather-pen or a brush dipped in a solution with iron in it, made from red-hot (oxidised) iron and sour palm wine. As soon as the solution came in contact with the tanning agent with which the cloth was impregnated the outline of the pattern emerged in black. When printing-blocks were used for this, the iron solution had to be thick enough for it to be transferred to the cloth. Then followed repeated 'boilings' and treatment in goat- or sheep-dung, the purpose of which was to remove every trace of tanning agent before the next process, the dyeing with indigo, began. The black outline of the design produced by the iron solution acted as a guide for the next stages of applying the wax-resist and painting with the colour-substance or mordant.

The indigo process began with the fabric being treated in rice-water, dried and again pounded to make it as smooth as possible. A resist wax-mixture (beeswax and resin) was applied with a brush to those parts that had to be protected from the blue dye; this is to say, the surfaces that later would stand out white or were dyed red. The wax was painted on one side only of the cloth, which was then laid briefly in the sun which made the wax penetrate to the other side. The cloth was then handed over to the blue-dyer, who in due course returned it dyed blue. The indigo-dyer used a large earthenware jar into which the cloth was put doubled with the outside facing out. There it was left for an hour and a half or so to be then taken out for oxidisation and rinsing. The fast-making process, so important for dyeing vegetable material with indigo, happens automatically in conjunction with the next stage in the procedure.

Once dyed blue, the cloth was ready for the most difficult stage of the entire procedure, dyeing red. First, however, all wax and resin had to be removed, and this was done in a series of strong boilings and treatment in sheep- and cow-dung, whereby the cloth was also prepared for the necessary treatment with fat buffalo-milk which preceded the actual dyeing. This procedure, which was of decisive significance for the end result, was performed with the utmost care. The milk was worked into the cloth using the hands, etc. Then, when everything necessary had been done, the cloth was taken to the red-dyer who often lived in quite a different place. In order to achieve a good result, the red-dyer needed access to a well with hard water (i.e. containing lime) which was not so easy to come by in India. Often in a town there has no more than a single such well.

The red-dye can be obtained from several kinds of Morinda or from the roots of a plant called chaia (*Oldenlandia umbellata*). These are used when dry and can still be bought by the bunch in the ordinary market. These chaia roots have to be finely pulverised in a stone mortar (wooden ones are considered quite unsuitable) before they are added to the dye-bath along with the careful addition of 'hard' water.

When a cotton fabric is dyed with madder, the process must not be carried out too hastily. The procedure begins with slight heat which is slowly increased. After some days' treatment the bath is allowed to boil for roughly an hour and then the fire is quenched. When the bath has cooled, the cloth is removed and allowed to drip-dry until the next day when it is washed and rinsed.

Sometimes certain parts of the design were given a yellow colour, especially when they wanted to make the leaves in a design green or greenish. The ingredients for the yellow dye include pomegranate peel, the flowers of the cadu-bush and alum. Unfortunately, this dye has little fastness and will normally disappear after four or five washes. The fastness can be enhanced by adding to it certain wax substances, but this can only be at the expense of the intensity of the colour. On the other hand, the red, and, above all, the blue shades remain with outstanding brightness in calico many hundreds of years old.

A dancing girl from Central Java wearing a batik-sarong with a *latar-puthi* design, that is to say white background and dark figuring. From Raffles *History of Java*, London 1817.

INDIGO BROWN

West African Kola-brown

In West Africa it is not unusual to come across fabrics with plangi-patterning in which the indigo colour has been combined with brown dye. The brown dye is obtained from finely pulverised kola- or guru-nuts from the kola tree (*Cola nitida*) which grows particularly in tropical Africa. The seeds, dried and pulverised, contain both a dye-stuff and a caffeine substance and so are often used as a stimulant. In the olden days they were also used to make ill-tasting water more drinkable and to dull sensations of hunger.

Javanese Soga-brown

Since a long time back the colours used in classic Javanese batik have been indigo-blue, the self-colours of the basic material, and a dark reddish brown. In Indonesia this brown dye-stuff has been obtained largely from different kinds of dye-wood, often the same as supplied the tanner with tanning agents. They are obtained by extraction from the bark or heartwood – rich in colouring compounds – of a number of tropical bushes and trees. The dye-wood colour used in the manufacture of batik comes from the soga-tree (*Peltophorum ferrogingeum*).

Batik work is usually dyed by laying it in a dye-bath, so large that the entire material is completely immersed, and leaving it there overnight. The material must be as flat as possible and must be turned now and then and kept in movement for a while in order to prevent it ending up looking 'veined'.

The colour you get if you dye without special additions is relatively weak and little able to stand up to washing. It takes a further subsequent treatment to achieve the right shade, the maximal saturation and a certain fastness to light and washing. In other words, the quality of the dyeing is directly dependent on the after work one puts upon it, and here good fixatives are especially valuable. One is told that in the old days Javanese women used to regard their special mixtures as family secrets, which they were very reluctant to reveal to outsiders. Such a recipe might well include alum, root-sugar, lemon juice and the buds of *Sophora japonica*, the latter of which contain quercitron – all in carefully weighed and measured quantities. This mixture has the ability to fix the dye. A combination of treatment with Turkish red oil and an alum bath has been shown also to possess great advantages. But whatever method of dyeing is used and what subsequent treatment applied, the brown-tones gradually fade and eventually disappear more or less completely. Old batik work can be worn down until the fibres begin to break, but will still retain the indigo-blue with almost its original depth of tone and lustre.

Woven picture by Kerstin Gustafsson. Woven of
handspun wool which has been dyed with
indigo in a variety of shades. The area is
40″ × 40″ (100 × 100 cm). The picture is the
property of Örebro Läns Landsting (Örebro
District Council).

INDIGO DYEING
TODAY

When dyeing with mordants there is normally no need to fear any really serious mishap provided you stick to the doses recommended for the chemicals and treat the textile in the proper way in the dye-bath. Dyeing with indigo however is, in important aspects, quite unlike other dyeing. An indigo-bath is almost a living creature and reacts swiftly and implacably to any disruption that may occur during the dyeing process, a fact that makes considerable demands on those in charge of it; calling in no small degree for the ability to involve oneself with the proceedings as well as the true craftsman's skills.

The recipe and instructions may be explicit and correct, but the unexpected and the irrational can still happen during dyeing and upset the balance of the chemicals, however well-balanced initially. This makes it more important to keep a closer watch on the condition of the solution than when using mordants. In my opinion, this fact makes it far more important, when dyeing with indigo, to understand the mechanism of dyeing than to rely on printed instructions that do not always foresee every eventuality. Problems may arise unless conditions are ideal; with which the dyer may not be able to deal unless he has considerable experience.

In the old days dyers had to rely mostly on the signals from their own senses when judging the condition of the bath during dyeing. Touch, smell and even taste helped to judge if and when the dyeing solution needed to be changed and how. It would be a considerable advantage if indigo-dyers could acquire some of the old knacks.

The Technique of Dyeing with Indigo

Reduction and oxidisation of the dye-stuff

Indigo dye, as we know, is insoluble in water, in contrast with mordant dyes – and therefore cannot dye a textile fibre directly, but must first be transformed into soluble form using what is called a reduction agent, some slightly alkaline fluid. After the material has been treated in the dye-bath, the indigo dye-stuff is restored by a reverse process, oxidisation, back into its insoluble form. It is then firmly anchored in the fibres, where it cannot be dislodged except by some extreme measure. Indigo that has been reduced to a fine powder and mixed with water to make a paste has a deep shade of blue, while the solution in the dye-bath in which the dye-stuff is dissolved is faintly yellowy green and clear.

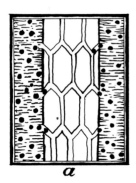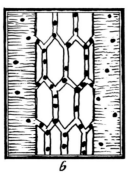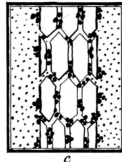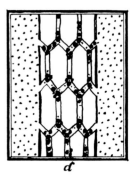

Diagram of the dyeing process.
a. Section of the fibre in water with reduced indigo in it
b. Water and the molecules of the dye-stuff penetrate the amorphous area of the fibres
c. The molecules of the dye have 'taken', impoverishing the solution to a corresponding degree.
d. The indigo has been turned back into its insoluble form by the oxygen in the air and is now imprisoned in the fibres.

Dye-baths for different fibres and techniques

Indigo, along with purple, is one of the very few natural dye-stuffs which can dye animal and vegetable fibres. Differences in their chemical structure, however, mean that the methods used in dyeing with them have to be adapted to the various kinds of fibre. Instructions for dyeing wool cannot be used for dyeing cotton without modification etc. There can be considerable variations within one and the same kind of fibre and these can have a profound effect both on the reception of the dye and on the final colour.

An indigo-bath that is to be used for different forms of resist-dyeing calls for a certain degree of technical adaptation. A bath well-suited to ikat streaky-dyeing can be quite unacceptable for a paste-resist printed fabric.

En
Upriktig och pålitelig

Färg=Bok,

Hwarefter
Hwar Hushållare kan färga
alla sina tilwärkningar och hwad
han behöfwer, på Ylle och Linne,
samt Bomullsgarn och
Silkes=Tyger.

Utgifwen til Allmänhetens Nytta.

Stockholm,
Tryckt uti Kongl. Tryckeriet
1 7 5 9.

Indigo recipes of yesterday and today

Indigo being one of the most valuable and most used textile dyes, the technical literature contains numerous recipes for its use. Some of the older recipes are reproduced at the end of this book (pp. 170–3) but most have been omitted, either because the suggested ingredients are no longer to be had, or because they are so poisonous – which today, makes them unacceptable.

A true and reliable Dye-book with which every householder will be able to dye all he manufactures and what he needs, on Wool and Linen, as well as cotton yarn and silk-cloth. Published for the common good. Stockholm. Printed in the Royal Printing Works 1759.

Relationship between dye, fibre and resist

INDIGO

ANIMAL FIBRES
wool, silk etc.

VEGETABLE FIBRES
cotton, linen, hemp etc.

yarn
loose wool
cloth
ikat-resist yarn

cloth
with
wax-resin
resist
(Batik)

cloth
with
paste-resist
(Blue-print)

cloth
without
resist
yarn with
ikat-resist

Low alkaline bath temperature 45°-55°C hydrogen sulphite solution with ammonia or urine

Moderately alkaline bath temperature 20°-24°C hydrogen sulphite solution with a modicum of lye

Alkaline bath temperature 20°-24°C green vitriol lime solution (or zinc lime)

Low alkaline bath temperature 20°-24°C minimum lye or green vitriol lime solution

Detail of Tunisian cloak woven with firmly twisted woollen yarn dyed indigo in two shades of deep blue. Area 4' (120 cm) square.

Dyeing Wool and Other

The hydrogen sulphite bath and its active factor

The recipes given in the book have all been adapted to craft dyeing with today's materials. For practical purposes they have been divided into those for cotton and wool, the two most important kinds of fibre that can be used for dyeing with indigo. The main recipes in either section have been tested in practice for a number of years.

The various ways in which the liquor for dyeing with indigo has been prepared have been described in the first part of this book. Though undoubtedly they worked well enough for those with a lifelong experience of their use and special techniques, most of them are more of historical, ethnographic interest than practical use. For those who dye with indigo today the important and most effective bath you can prepare is one with hydrogen sulphite solution. For this you begin by making a concentrated solution of the dye (stock solution), which is then added to a larger bath (blank bath) into which certain requisite chemicals have already been placed in readiness. The two solutions, now united, comprise the bath liquor in which dyeing can take place. The advantage in having a stock solution of the dye-stuff is that this makes it easy to add more indigo to the bath, if for any reason this should be required.

The procedure for dyeing woollen materials in a hydrogen sulphite bath is briefly as follows:

a　　　*b*　　　*c*

Animal Fibres with Indigo

a. The indigo dye-stuff is dissolved at 122–131°F (50–55°C) in a small quantity of water with the help of caustic soda (lye) and sodium hydrosulphite to produce the stock solution.

b. The larger amount of water is heated to 113–131°F (45–55°C) with lime solution, ammonia, sodium hydrosulphite and salt added to become the blank bath.

c. The basic liquor is added to the blank bath making a dye-bath (indigo).

d. The wool (yarn or cloth) is introduced and worked in the bath.

e. The wool is lifted out and the blue allowed to oxidise out.

f. If a deeper shade is required, the stuff being dyed is returned to the bath.

g. The process stops when the colour of the required depth has been achieved. The blue is oxidised out.

h. Rinsing, washing and neutralising, plus drying, conclude the procedure.

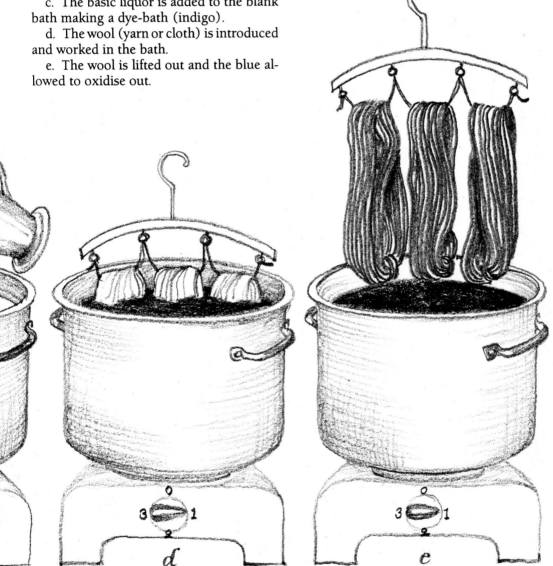

d   e

Woollen yarn spun by hand by Kerstin Gustafsson using wool from her own sheep and then dyed with indigo.

Pullovers designed and knitted by Lena Nordström.

The wool used in that on the right has been dyed with indigo, madder and cochineal. The left-hand one was dyed with indigo, moss and bog-myrtle that has been darkened with green vitriol.

A. Recipe for a stock bath of varying quantities but same strength

Water 122°F (50°C)	2 fl oz (50 ml)	6 fl oz (165)	18 fl oz (500)
Indigo	½ tsp (3 g)	2 tsp (10 g)	6 tsp (30 g)
Caustic soda (lye) 25%	1 tsp (5 ml)	1 tbsp (16 ml)	3 tbsp (50 ml)
Sodium hydrosulphite	½ tsp (3 g)	2 tsp (10 g)	6 tsp (30 g)
(Ethyl alcohol optional)			

1 Work out and note down your quantities

2 Weigh out the dye and add water at 55°C

3 Measure out and add caustic soda lye

4 Measure out and add hydrosulphite

Recipe and

Preparation of the stock bath

The powdered indigo is mixed with part of the recommended quantity of water or ethyl alcohol in a glass or stainless steel vessel to make a thin dough. The rest of the warm water, the lye and, lastly, the hydrosulphite are added, stirring gently all the while, the hydrosulphite being sprinkled in to prevent its becoming lumpy. Use a glass rod to stir and see that no undissolved pigment collects on the bottom.

This stock solution is then poured into a glass vessel with a close-fitting lid and placed in the water-bath at about 122° F (50° C) for 60 minutes, if using natural indigo, and about 15 minutes, if using synthetic indigo. The liquor will gradually acquire a yellow brown colour and a streak of it on a glass plate should turn blue within a minute.

The recipes given above are all of the same strength but for different quantities. They can be used for all dye recipes which include indigo. Put into the blank bath as much of the stock solution as you reckon will achieve the depth of colour you wish. (See the table for altering the solution on page 123.) The rest of the liquor can be kept for quite a long time if, each time some has been taken out, you fill up the space with glass balls, so that there is as little air above the surface of the liquor as possible.

If larger amounts are to be dyed, larger quantities of liquor than suggested here can be made, just multiply the quantities given by, say, ten.

Instructions for a Hydrogen Sulphite Bath

B. Recipe for a blank bath

Water at 122° F (50° C)	5 quarts (5 litres)	10 quarts (10 litres)
Solution of lime	1 tbsp (12.5 ml)	2 tbsp (25 ml)
Powdered gelatine	$\frac{1}{4}$ tsp (1–2 g)	$\frac{1}{2}$ tsp (2–4 g)
Ammonia 25% (without hydrogen sulphite)	1 fl oz (30 ml)	2 fl oz (60 ml)
Sodium hydrosulphite	$\frac{1}{2}$ tsp (2.5 g)	1 tsp (5 g)
Salt (for darker shades)	$1\frac{3}{4}$–$3\frac{1}{2}$ oz (50–100 g)	$3\frac{1}{2}$–7 oz (100–200 g)

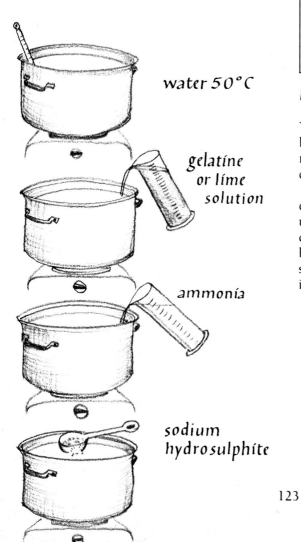

water 50°C

gelatine or lime solution

ammonia

sodium hydrosulphite

Preparation of the blank bath

Dissolve the ingredients in the warm water in the order given in the recipe, using a pail or other receptacle of stainless steel, or even plastic, kept warm in a water-bath.

Basic liquor (for 5 or 10 blank baths)

Depth of tone	5 quarts (5 litres)	10 quarts (10 litres)
Deep-blue to black-blue	$2\frac{1}{2}$ fl oz (75 ml)	5 fl oz (150 ml)
Full strength to deep-blue	$1\frac{1}{2}$ tbsp (25 ml)	3 tbsp (50 ml)
Medium to full strength blue	$\frac{1}{2}$ tbsp (7.5 ml)	1 tbsp (15 ml)
Light to medium blue	($\frac{1}{2}$ tsp) (2.5 ml)	(1 tsp) (5 ml)

Preparation of the dye-bath

The dye-bath is prepared by adding to the blank bath that quantity of stock solution necessary to achieve the desired depth of colour, see above.

A bath of 10 qt (10 l) should be able to dye 10 oz (300 g) of yarn at a time and in all up to 10 hanks of 3.5 oz (100 g) each can be dealt with without adding solution to the bath. The stock solution should be carefully stirred, measuring it into the glass measuring jar. It may be desirable to warm it up, if

Dyeing in an indigo bath, a picture taken in
Kano, the dyers' town of Northern Nigeria.
Visible on the surface of the bath are the
characteristic blue-violet bubbles, the so-called
'bloom'. Today, as the picture shows, dyers wear
rubber gloves to protect their hands from the
chemicals in the bath. In the old days they wore
goatskin gloves, or so Ismail said (page 60).

there is any sediment of pigment. The solution should turn a clear yellowy-green after a short while and the dark-blue bubbles (bloom) will appear on the surface or along the side of the vessel.

If the actual dyeing has to be interrupted for any reason, the bath's surface must be well covered with a sheet of plastic to prevent the oxygen in the air spoiling the bath.

Working in the dye-bath

Before dyeing can begin, the skin or bloom formed on the surface of the bath by the re-oxidised dye-stuff has to be removed. The material, that has been wetted-out and squeezed out, is immersed in the bath and worked for about 10 minutes. In doing this it is important as far as possible to avoid mixing air into the bath, since the oxygen in it will oxidise part of the dye-stuff and precipitate it in the bath itself without its attaching to the fibres. Thus, when dyeing with indigo, rods cannot be used to move the yarn about. Instead, it is worked by moderate movements and careful turning while seeing that it does not float up to the surface.

After about 10 minutes the yarn is lifted out and the dye allowed to oxidise out for at least 10 minutes. For the first minute or two the hanks should be kept close enough to the surface of the bath so that the surplus liquid can run off without creating too much foam. The characteristic change in colour from yellowy-green to blueish now occurs spontaneously, and will be speeded up if the strands are spread out so that air can reach the inner parts of the hank. The worse, i.e. poor in oxygen, the air is in the dye-works, the slower will be the process, and vice versa.

Multi-dipping

Where a deeper and darker shade than that first obtained is required, the process can be repeated as soon as the colour from the first dip has fully oxidised out. However, this should not really be repeated more than four times and for 5 minutes each time. If the colour is still not strong enough even then, it will be better to top up with stock solution than to continue dipping. The process of oxidisation puts a certain strain on the fibres and so should not be repeated more often than necessary.

It is important to keep the temperature of the bath constant, between 113–131°F (45–55°C).

125

Control and adjustment of the dye-bath

An indigo bath has something of the complexity of a gothic cathedral, but it is also very vulnerable. Damage to just one part can have dire consequences for the whole. Even if one is aware of the special requirements of dyeing with indigo, there is no avoiding the bath gradually deteriorating. Especially after repeated dipping or the immersion of material that is porous and thus harbours a lot of air, the strain on the solution is considerable. All the hydrosulphite is gradually used up, and products of oxidisation are formed with the result that the lye too gradually becomes ineffective.

Someone with experience will soon see the characteristic signs of the bath reaching the point of 'dying', as it used to be called. Its limpidity diminishes and it becomes blueish and cloudy, as the chemicals in it are oxidised and the indigo dye-stuff precipitates. The bath can then be 'sharpened' by adding as much ammonia and hydrosulphite as was first put into the blank bath. Dyeing can be resumed as soon as the bath has recovered its correct appearance.

It is possible to check with phenolphthalein paper that the correct amount of ammonia has been put in. In an indigo-bath this strip of white paper should not turn more than pink, indicating a pH value of about 7.5–8. An overdose of ammonia produces a strong violet hue. Postpone dyeing for a bit and check again, for the surplus tends to evaporate relatively quickly.

Because the composition and life of an indigo-bath depends so greatly on a correct pH-balance, it is important to see that the material to be dyed is as neutral as possible when it enters the bath. Under no circumstances may it be acid. A test with indicator paper should therefore be made on a part of the fibre material that has been moistened, preferably with distilled water, before it is immersed in the dye-bath.

How to measure the pH value

All processes of dyeing and printing with indigo and related processes depend to a greater or lesser extent on a well-balanced pH. It is thus valuable for each individual process to try to obtain and maintain the most suitable and best functioning pH value. Here special test papers are most useful.

Phenolphthalein-paper is white but changes to red-violet if dipped into a bath with a relatively high pH, that is to say 7 and over (see page 127).

Red litmus paper turns blue in alkaline conditions.

Blue litmus paper turns red when conditions are acid. The change takes place at pH 7.

Universal test paper is easiest to handle and can be bought in practically every chemist's shop. Dip a piece in the solution to be tested and its yellow colour will change to red or blue depending on how strongly acid or alkaline it is. Then, by comparing this with a separate colour scale you get an idea of its approximate pH value. This simple test, which is quickly made, often provides support for the inexperienced dyer who is feeling uncertain when faced with an indigo-bath suspected of failing. The indicator paper's scale ranges from 1–10, 1 being the most strongly acid (= red), 7–8 are neutral or very faintly alkaline (= yellow-green – green) and, finally, 10 is faintly alkaline to alkaline (= blue).

pH table

with the different notations for acidity and alkalinity

Increasing alkalinity	↑ 14	most strongly alkaline
	13	
	12	strongly alkaline
	11	moderately alkaline
	10	
	9	faintly alkaline
Neutral point	8	
	7	neutral point
	6	
	5	faintly acid
	4	
	3	acid
	2	
Increasing acidity	1	strongly acid
	↓ 0	most strongly acid

The different pH values in the above table are arranged from 0–14 which includes all practically possible degrees of acid- and alkali-content in, say, a dye-bath. In ordinary parlance one speaks of increasing or decreasing pH value, meaning thereby the increase or decrease in the value of the figure in the scale. When the pH value is increasing, the degree of acidity of the bath decreases, reaching the neutral point of pH = 7. Above pH = 7 (8–14) lies the alkaline (basic) area and alkalinity increases as the pH value rises so that pH = 14 denotes the strongest alkalinity.

Subsequent treatment

Rinsing, washing, soaping
Yarn dyed with indigo has to be carefully rinsed and washed once dyeing has been completed. This is partly in order to remove the strong alkali used in the bath and to get rid of any remaining dye-pigment from the surface of the fibres. Under no circumstances may the bath-liquid be allowed to dry on the yarn, since this concentrates the caustic soda (lye) on the fibres making them stiff and so risking their becoming brittle.

The yarn is washed in tepid water with a suitable quantity of a fine washing material and is rinsed until the water runs away uncoloured. Finally it is rinsed in clean water with enough acetic acid added to give it a distinct sour taste. This final treatment increases its fastness and restores the wool's elasticity.

Woven material dyed with indigo can be given extra fastness, above all a better fastness to rubbing, by the so-called soaping process. The material is worked in a water-bath to which has been added a neutral washing agent for about 20 minutes. The temperature should not exceed 122°F (50°C).

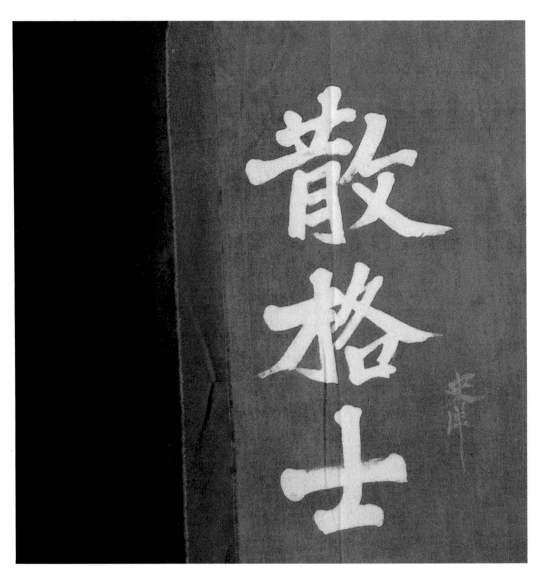

The author's name in Chinese characters drawn by Jan Sisefsky. The characters were painted on cotton by the batik-technique using a brush. Synthetic wax and paraffin in equal quantities were used. The cotton was dyed in an indigo (hydrogen sulphite) bath. The first dip used $\frac{1}{4}$ tsp per quart (1 gram per litre). More stock solution was added with every dip according to its appearance. There were eight dips in all. The picture also shows two pieces of cotton of different quality which received the same treatment, but were better able to take up the colour.

Dyeing Cotton and Other Vegetable Fibres with Indigo

There are good reasons why in this book such a clear distinction has been made between dyeing wool with indigo and dyeing cotton, linen etc. with the same dye. Thanks to differences in the ability of the different fibres to take up the dye, and the variations in their resistance to the chemicals that have to be used, both the recipes and the methods of dyeing are quite different. Another, not unimportant reason, is that both kinds of fibre have come to be used for textiles that are subsequently patterned by quite different techniques, such as ikat/streaky yarn, batik and paste-resist blue-print, which require different procedures in dyeing.

The difference between dyeing cotton with indigo compared with using it to dye wool, is that during the dipping phase a given amount of cotton will take up far less of the indigo in the bath than would the corresponding quantity of wool. The slow speed at which the dissolved indigo is taken up means that a state of equilibrium between the quantity of indigo absorbed by the fibres and that which the solution releases is quickly achieved. Thus the colour obtained cannot be strengthened by prolonging the period of working, as is possible when using other natural dye-stuffs.

Multi-dipping

The strength of the indigo colour is instead achieved by repeated immersion and oxidisation, whereby the small quantity of indigo that each dip attaches to the fibres is added to previous amounts. This procedure can be continued until the required depth of hue has been achieved. Repeated immersion does not harm the cotton fibres to the same extent as it would damage wool fibres.

This procedure assumes that the indigo which is oxidised out in the fibres is not allowed to return to the solution when the material is returned to the bath. Thus, there are several things to remember: (a) The dye-bath must be kept cool (68–75°F or 20–24°C) throughout the dyeing process; (b) Alkalinity and content of hydrosulphite should be kept as low as possible, considerably lower than when dyeing wool; and this means adding no more than will just keep the indigo dissolved; (c) The dips must be brief, about 1 minute, except for the first which can last 5–10 minutes to give good equalisation; (d) Oxidisation between dips must be as complete as possible, which means it should last at least 5 minutes where there is a good draught. Widths of cloth that are hung up on a rack should be spread out and strands in skeins of yarn separated so that the oxygen in the air can reach the inner parts; (e) The lime-water (gelatine) is of great importance because it counteracts the tendency of the dissolved indigo to precipitate in the bath and so become inactive.

A. Recipe for a stock solution
(different quantities – same strength)

Water at 122°F (50°C)	2 fl oz (50 ml)	6 fl oz (165)	18 fl oz (500)
Indigo	½ tsp (3 g)	2 tsp (10 g)	6 tsp (30 g)
Sodium hydroxide	1 tsp (5 ml)	1 tbsp (16 ml)	3 tbsp (50 ml)
Sodium hydrosulphite	½ tsp (3 g)	2 tsp (10 g)	6 tsp (30 g)
(Ethyl alcohol optional)			

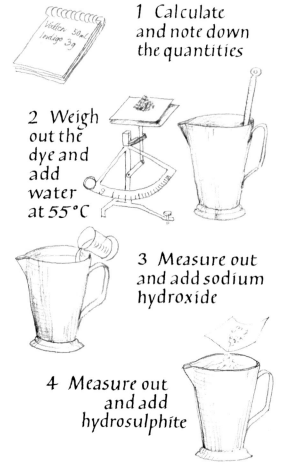

1 Calculate and note down the quantities

2 Weigh out the dye and add water at 55°C

3 Measure out and add sodium hydroxide

4 Measure out and add hydrosulphite

Recipe and

Preparation of stock solution

The powdered indigo dye-stuff is mixed in a vessel made of glass or stainless steel with some of the water required (or with ethyl alcohol) until it makes a thin paste. Then the rest of the warm water, the lye and the hydrosulphite are added, in that order, the hydrosulphite being sprinkled on so that it does not form lumps. Stir carefully with a glass rod and make sure that no undissolved pigment collects on the bottom of the vessel.

This stock solution is then poured into a glass jar with a close-fitting lid and placed in a bath of water at around 122°F (50°C) for 10 minutes when using natural indigo and for about 15 minutes if using synthetic indigo. The solution gradually takes on a yellow-brown shade. A sample drop or two spread on a glass plate with a glass rod should turn blue within a minute.

The three recipes given are all of equal strength, but for different quantities. They can be used for all dye recipes in which indigo figures. Add to your blank bath what you reckon will be enough of the stock solution to achieve the depth of colour you want. (See the table on p. 123 for the quantities.) The rest of the solution can be kept for quite a long time, if every time some of it is taken out, this is replaced with glass balls so that the amount of air above the surface of the solution is as small as possible.

If larger quantities of material are to be dyed, you can make larger quantities of the stock solution than have been suggested here; in which case multiply the quantities given in the recipe above by ten or whatever is necessary.

Instructions for a Hydrogen Sulphite Bath

B. Recipe for a blank bath

Water at 68–75°F	5 quarts (5 litres)	10 quarts (10 litres)
20–24°C (rainwater or softened)		
Lime water 10% or gelatine solution	1 tbsp (12.5 ml)	2 tbsp (25 ml)
Sodium hydroxide (caustic soda)	¼ tsp (1 ml)	½ tsp (2 ml)
Sodium hydrosulphite	¼ tsp (1–2 g)	½ tsp (2–3 g)
Salt	3½ oz (100 g)	7 oz (200 g)

Preparation of the blank bath

Dissolve the ingredients in the order given here, remembering that here ammonia has been replaced by sodium hydroxide (caustic soda) and the solution has to be cold.

C. Amount of stock solution added when dyeing cotton

	5 quarts (5 litres)	10 quarts (10 litres)
Light shades	1 tsp (5 ml)	2 tsp (10 ml)
Medium light shades	1½ tbsp (25 ml)	3 tbsp (50 ml)
Dark shades	4 fl oz (125 ml)	8 fl oz (250 ml)

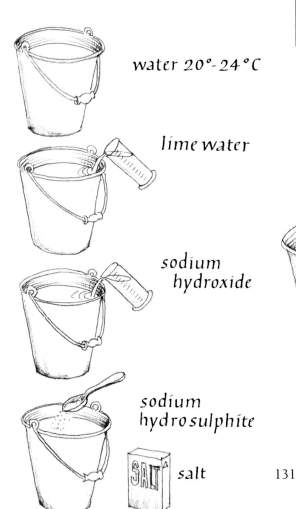

water 20°-24°C

lime water

sodium hydroxide

sodium hydrosulphite

salt

indigo solution

Preparation of the dye-bath

The principle of the indigo-bath for cotton is the same as that for wool, i.e. a certain quantity of the stock solution is added to the blank bath, the whole is then carefully stirred so that the two mix properly; after which you can begin working the material to be dyed. The above table will provide a guide as to how much of the stock solution should be added to the other, but this is no substitute for actual experience, still less for the always important test-dyeings that should always precede any major undertaking. The strength (or depth of colour) of the final result depends on two factors:

   a. the amount of stock solution added to the blank bath, and

   b. the number of dips into the bath.

Checking and adjusting the bath

The bath must be continually checked, as has to be done when dyeing wool (p. 126). When deep shades are required and many dips necessary, the bath can become impoverished, even before enough colour has been built up. The signs of this are that the colour of the bath changes, the characteristic floating patches of 'bloom' with its iridescent blue-violet bubbles disappear, and a further dip does not result in any deepening of the colour. This may call for the addition of more of the stock solution and the bath can be sharpened by adding lye and hydrosulphite ($\frac{1}{4}$ tsp per 10qt: 1 ml or 1 g per 10 l of solution). Test with indicator paper to make sure that the solution maintains a pH value of around 9–10.

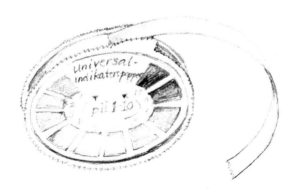

Subsequent Treatment of Dyed Material

Rinsing, washing

Material dyed with indigo must be carefully rinsed and washed when dyeing is finished. Soap flakes or synthetic washing materials free of bleaching agents or optical white should be used.

Soaping

Soaping is more important when dyeing cotton than when dyeing wool, since the fastness to light of the two is not the same. It is especially important when light shades are produced. The yarn or material is worked in a bath of water at 185–194°F (85–90°C), perhaps with some washing material added. The hardening of the colour brought about by soaping also makes the indigo somewhat more reddish.

Souring

A well-known feature of yarn or cloth that has been dyed with indigo is that it does not always stand up to rubbing satisfactorily. This is not always so to the same degree, for much depends on what type of bath was used, the reduction agent employed, how well the whole process went and what preliminary and subsequent treatment was given. One method that has been used since olden days is to work the material in a weak acid bath after dyeing. This is doubly beneficial for material that has been resist-printed, because the acid also restores the material's original whiteness to those parts of the pattern which the copper salts in the paste may have discoloured, making them a greeny-yellow. Acetic acid is often used for souring, being added to the rinsing bath until it has a strong acid taste. Carl Sahlin has described how in the dye-works at Vollsjö 'once the yarn has reached the desired darker or lighter blue colour, it was neutralised in a large vessel with water to which a tumbler of sulphuric acid per bundle of yarn was added, so as to make it free of grease, after which it was wrung out, dried and was ready'.

The old recipes for blue-printing and blue-dyeing often recommend sulphuric acid for souring, but as there is a risk of this exploding if improperly handled, this book everywhere recommends acetic acid instead. This is somewhat more expensive, but just as effective and less risky.

NB If sulphuric acid is used, be careful that dilution is achieved by adding small quantities at a time, stirring all the while, and that the *acid is poured into the water and never the water into the acid.*

Causes of Failure

Quality of the dye-stuff (indigo) below par, e.g. a low concentration of indigo-blue. (See p. 134.)

Reducing agent (using hydrosulphite) more or less ineffective, usually because it is too old. (Seè p. 137.)

Addition of chemicals not made in the prescribed order when the stock solution or blank bath was prepared. Hydrosulphite added *after* the lye. (See p. 122.)

Some substance being forgotten; e.g. lime water or gelatine, salt.

The stock solution being in a bad condition, i.e. the dye-stuff is no longer in solution. Cure by heating to around 122°F (50°C) and adding hydrosulphite.

The textile material (yarn, cloth) not being properly wetted-out, and so might contain grease, vegetable matter etc. or be too acid.

Continuous checking of the bath not being carried out. (See pages 126 and 132.)

Defective quality of the water. (See page 139.)

Dye too weak. The reasons for this can be (a) too little of the stock solution put in, page 125; (b) too few dips into the bath, pages 125 and 129; (c) bad stock solution or inferior dye-stuff, page 126.

Dye too deep, can be because too much stock solution has been added.
NB Dilution is done with liquid from the blank bath, not just with water.

Uneven and streaky dyeing can be due to inadequate working of the material in the bath. (See page 125.)

Uneven dyeing of cloth can be caused by unintentional resist, i.e. the cloth has remained folded too long during dyeing.

Uneven dyeing of yarn can be due to its not having been wetted-out before being placed in the bath.

Testing for fastness to light of yarn dyed with an indigo solution, coerulignone or oleum, which on the Continent is called Saxon blue. The method by which the indigo is dissolved in a bath of smoking sulphuric acid was recommended in practically every book on vegetable dyes from 1900 to 1960. However, the German and English dyer's handbooks early warned against the use of this blue as that which 'gives the least fastness'. (H. Schrader, fine-dyer in Hamburg, 1833).

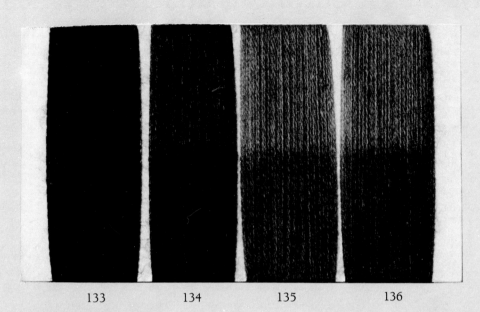

133   134   135   136

133 Cochineal + indigo
134 Cochineal + indigo
135 Cochineal + madder + indigo
136 Madder with blue vitriol + indigo

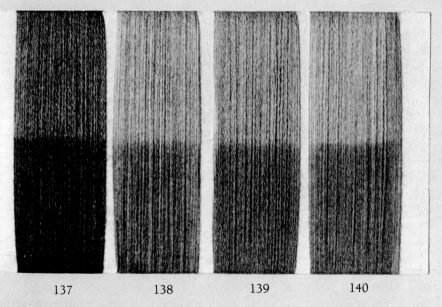

137   138   139   140

137 Indigo
138 Indigo
139 Birch leaves + indigo
140 Bog myrtle + indigo

Dye-stuffs, Chemicals and Textile Aids

Chemical formula for natural and synthetic indigo

Natural indigo

From the 17th century up to the beginning of this century natural indigo came in the form of lumps that had to be ground before they could be used. They were hard and light in weight and the surface was a pretty matt blue. Cracks and broken surfaces showed up copper-red and, if the quality of the indigo was good, had a gloss.

Today, natural indigo is sold, where you are lucky enough to find it, in the form of a fine powder or granules, and has a smell that the experienced indigo-dyer will easily recognise.

Good indigo can contain up to 80 per cent indigo-blue, the rest being glue-substances and impurities. The quality of indigo has always varied considerably according to its country of origin and how it has been produced. Recently indigo of un-warrantably low concentration has been sold misleadingly as 'genuine natural indigo'. Many disappointed dyers, faced with hanks of faintly grey-blue yarn, now know that the description gave no guarantee of high quality.

Synthetic indigo

Synthetic indigo comes as a powder or granulated and is of high uniform quality. Its composition is the same as natural indigo, as can be seen in the diagram above. The difference between the two lies in the absence of impurities and substances that contribute nothing to the dyeing process. The term 'synthetic' is not correct in this respect and should have been replaced long ago with a more adequate label.

Ammonia

Caustic ammonia, salmiac spirit H_3N or H_4NOH

A solution of ammonia gas in water is used for its alkaline qualities in the dyeing of woollen materials with indigo. It takes the place of sodium hydroxide (caustic soda) in the blank bath, as it is kinder to the fibres and can evaporate as gas during drying. As it evaporates easily it must be stored in a tightly closed vessel and kept in a cool place.

Gelatine

Specially prepared bone glue can profitably be substituted for other glues in the indigo-bath. Because quality is high the quantity can be reduced by half that of other glues. It can be dissolved directly in the bath. See under Glue on page 137.

Green vitriol

Vitriol, ferrosulphate $FeSO_4$, $7H_2O$
Greenish, fairly large crystals sometimes with a brownish discoloration. As green vitriol disintegrates in warm air, it must be kept in a cool, not too dry place. It is used when dyeing cotton (blue-print) in a 'vitriol-lime bath'.

Lime, burnt

Calcium oxide CaO
It is used as the alkaline additive to 'green-vitriol-lime' baths. It must be handled with care as it is corrosive. If it splashes onto your eyes, bathe them at once in plenty of water and inform your doctor. Wear protective clothing. (If slaked lime is handy increase the quantity by one-third.)

Glue

Joiner's glue, cologne glue etc.
A natural albuminous substance obtained by boiling up bone, remnants of leather etc. It is used, among other things, in retarding the speedy precipitation of a dye-substance in a dye-bath and to protect wool fibres against the alkali in the bath. It is added to the blank bath as a 10% solution prepared using 2 tsp (10 g) glue to every 4 fl oz (100 ml) of hot water. To increase fastness some preservative should be added.

Sodium hydrosulphite

Sodium hyposulphite $Na_2S_2O_4$
A fine white powder with a not entirely pleasant smell. It is a strong reduction agent used for vat-dyeing in most indigo-dyeing at the present time. It must be stored in a tightly closed vessel, but even so it will gradually deteriorate owing to air and damp. Once it has lost its characteristic smell, it is no longer usable. Avoid drops of water from measuring spoons etc. getting into the tin of hydrosulphite as this can generate heat and there is a risk of spontaneous combustion.

Sodium hydroxide

Caustic soda $NaOH$ (lye)
Comes in various guises: as hard white sticks, tablets or flakes that look like solid paraffin. It dissolves in water and in doing so generates a lot of heat. The solution, which is strongly alkaline, is called soda-lye and is used in the dye-bath for indigo. Because of the risks involved in handling solid caustic soda, it is recommended that a 25% solution of the lye should be used instead. (The recipes given in this book assume its use.)

Potash

Potassium hydroxide. Potassium carbonate K_2CO_3

A fine, white powder with a mildly alkaline action. Formerly produced solely by soaking vegetable or wood ash, when its quality depended on the basic material. The best 'potash burners' of Sweden used to use beechwood exclusively as this gave a purer product than any other wood.

Those who today wish to dye or print using the old recipes, which often include potash among the ingredients, must remember that today's corresponding product (with the same name) is considerably stronger. Therefore use a quarter or even an eighth of the amount recommended in the recipe.

If you would like to make your own potash, take 1 pint (5 dl) of beech-ash to each 10 pints (5 litres) of water, and let them stand for 1–2 days, after which the clear liquid is poured off and bottled or put in plastic containers. *NB* Label distinctly. Test its pH value with indicator papers (9–10 depending on the ash used).

Salt

Cooking salt, rock salt, sea salt, sodium chloride, NaCl

A white crystalline powder used to accelerate and encourage the attachment of indigo to the fibres, especially with strong dyes. The value of salt as a textile aid is mentioned in the most ancient sources.

Spirit

Ethyl alcohol, C_2H_5OH

This makes it easier for the dye-bath to soak the fibres, even if these are greasy or the attachment of dye to the fibres is otherwise hampered. It is especially important in dyeing cotton yarn (e.g. ikat). Hanks or warp-coils are soaked with the spirit, the surplus is then squeezed out (it can be used again) and the yarn, which is still damp, is put straight into the bath.

Spirit is sometimes used when indigo powder is being stirred into a stock solution where it hastens the process of solution. Spirits that one drinks may be used in an emergency and will have the same effect!

Zinc powder, zinc dust

Used as a reducing agent. It has to be handled with extreme care as it becomes explosive when mixed with air.

Acetic acid

Vinegar, acetone CH_3COOH

A weak liquid acid with a characteristic smell. Used mainly for rinsing dyed woollen yarn or for souring resist-printed cloths (blue-print). The best way of testing the right concentration is by tasting the solution. Enough should be added to the rinsing bath to give it a strong sour taste.

138

Urine, chamber lye

This is the secretion from the kidneys that that great observer and writer of antiquity, Pliny, mentions as one of the greatest aids of a Roman dyer. Its secretion is usually acid (pH about 6), but, depending on the foodstuffs that have been eaten (e.g. greens rich in basics), it can be alkaline.

Urine that is allowed to stand for some time gradually develops micro-organisms whose metabolism produces the ammonia which is a necessary reducing-agent for an indigo dye-bath (fermentation-bath). The old instructions for dyeing emphasise, and rightly, that the urine should be old, indeed, the older the better, according to recipe 43 in the book Rosetti wrote in 1540. The instructions given as to the quantities of urine suitable for a dye-bath contain one or two cryptic modifications: first, the requirement that it must be *human* urine, not only that, but, also. it must come from men, of which the most suitable is that from men who consume alcohol or, as the Swede, Cajsa Warg, puts it in her book of 1762 'those who have drunk strong drink'. With all due respect for that author's undoubted practical experience, one is entitled to wonder why urine from animals, women and people who do not drink 'strong drink' should not serve equally well.

Perhaps, we shall never know the answer, but we do know that urine, whatever its form, was the aid that for thousands of years made dyeing with indigo possible. It was only in our time that new preparations have replaced the traditional and always obtainable natural product.

Water

Water distributed by our water authorities, like water from our rivers and streams, has hitherto been perfectly serviceable both for dyeing and the other processes associated with it. However, the irresponsible exploitation of our natural resources that has been going on and is now damaging the environment to an extent that is affecting us all in different ways, is among others spoiling the water in our lakes and watercourses and its quality can no longer be taken for granted.

Certain places, indeed whole areas, may have water that contains ferrous impurities which affect the outcome of dyeing to a greater or lesser extent. Other places are encumbered with 'hard' water, i.e. water with calcium salts dissolved in it, the latter which can precipitate the indigo dye-stuff in the dye-bath. This results in pigment being left on the surface of the fibres, which then have extremely poor resistance to rubbing. However, there are various toughening substances that can make the calcium salts inoperative.

Where the quality of the water is extremely poor, it is best to use rain water, which can be collected in tanks and filtered before use. Melted snow also provides suitable water, but remembering the pollution of our air, both rain and melted snow should be allowed to fall for some time before it is collected. In other words, it is now necessary to cleanse the atmosphere a bit before these can be collected.

Chemicals and Aids for Resist-pastes

Alginate

Sodium alginate, Na alginate (sodium salt of alginic acid)

A natural product obtained from algae used as a thickening agent. A suitable consistency is obtained by dissolving 2 tsp (10 g) of alginate in 4 fl oz (100 ml) of water.

Balsam turpentine

French turpentine – wood turpentine

A solvent obtained by dry-distillation of various woods, which is used in some of the older recipes for paste. Not to be confused with mineral turpentine, a product of petroleum.

Beeswax

Obtained by melting down the combs of wax that bees build in which to rear their grubs and store their honey and pollen. It should be free of honey and foreign substances and any water in it dispelled by heating. It is used on its own or in conjunction with resin as a mechanical resist.

Sugar of lead

Pb Lead acetate (CH_3COO_2)

Colourless transparent crystals with a sweetish astringency. A usual component of resist-pastes in the 19th century and early part of the 20th century. It is *poisonous* and should be handled with extreme caution!

Glycerine

A thick, colourless, odourless liquid discovered by the Swedish chemist, Scheele, in 1779, which is used to hinder cracking of the surface of the resist.

Gum arabic

A preparation obtained from certain species of acacia consisting of white to brownish grains that are soluble in water. It is used as a thickening in pastes. It is a substance that was known in antiquity.

Resin

Secreted by conifers. When fresh it is more or less liquid, but gradually congeals into firm brown pieces. It is used in conjunction with beeswax as a mechanical resist with considerable power to withstand the effects of the dye-bath.

Kaolin: china clay

White or grey-white powder of aluminium silicate. It is the most common filling matter in pastes.

Carbamide $H_2N \cdot CO \cdot NH_2$

An agent for delaying drying (a urine substance) used in painting on paste or when printing with colour-yielding paste.

Copper acetate

Spanish green. $Cu(OH)CH_3COO$

Blue-green crystals only partially soluble in water, but wholly soluble in dilute acids. It is used to build a protective layer in resist-pastes in conjunction with green vitriol. *Poisonous!*

Green vitriol

Copper sulphate, Blue-stone, $CuSO_4 \cdot 5H_2O$

Blue crystals soluble in water, commonly used the world over to build a protective layer of paste.

Tallow

Tallow is a hard, somewhat brittle, white to yellowish fatty substance obtained from cattle, sheep and goats. Used as a mostly mechanical protection in various compositions of paste.

Lard, the rendered fat of pigs, is used both to give consistency to paste and as a mechanically active substance in it.

Rice-flour

An excellent thickening for pastes.

Handling and Storing of Chemicals

Many chemicals are gradually destroyed by humid air (sodium hydrosulphite and green vitriol are examples); thus chemicals in solid form should be kept dry in containers with close-fitting lids of plastic or bakelite. *NB* Vessels in which chemicals are stored should always be properly labelled. Old labels must be removed and not just have the words on them crossed out. Tins or bottles whose appearance suggests that

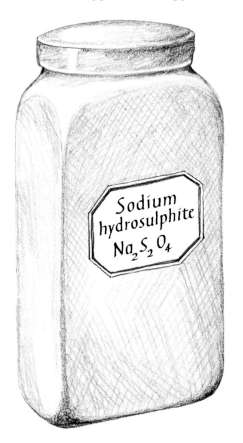

they contain edibles, beer or soft drinks should not be used. Obviously they should be stored where they are inaccessible to children, preferably in a locked cupboard, but in no circumstances in a pantry, food-store or similar place.

Concentrated acids and alkalis (e.g. caustic soda and burnt lime) corrode textiles, the skin, mucous membrane, and, especially, the eyes. Spots of acid or alkali on the skin and clothes should be washed off at once with water. *If a chemical gets into your eyes, you must bathe them immediately with plenty of water.* It would be advisable to go to a casualty department after doing so.

Protection of the environment

From the point of view of the environment, indigo-dyeing is not harmful to any real extent. Indeed, because it uses a bath that is more or less strongly alkaline, it can be said to give certain corrective substances back into our acidified nature. Nonetheless, we should perhaps bear in mind the advice given to dyers in Johan Linder's *Svenska Färge-Konst*, which was published in 1720: 'Water for dyeing should be fresh. River water is the best, then drip-water (rain water). Water containing saltpetre and lime-water are no use. That water is best in which shelled peas are cooked. Therefore can you dye very well in Leyden in Holland, because the river Rhône flows through the middle of the town.'

Workshop, Equipment and Tools

The dyeing with indigo of woollen and cotton materials differs in several respects and the methods used have to be suitably adapted. The handling of dyed goods, yarn or cloth, also calls for quite distinct dyeing processes. If they are to function well, an indigo-dyer's workshop, equipment and tools must have regard to:

a. *Its scope*, i.e. whether his is a small-scale undertaking mostly for his personal use, or whether he is working on a larger scale for a group of customers.

b. *The basic material* (type of fibre) – whether this is mainly of animal or vegetable origin.

c. *The type of final product*, i.e. whether it is mostly loose wool, yarn or cloth he is going to dye.

Room for dyeing with a hot-bath

Indigo-dyeing of wool and yarn of animal origin in a hot-bath will normally not require a room of any special design. Access to water, drainage and heating are obviously advantageous, especially if larger quantities are to be dyed at the same time. A stove with an output which can be regulated is specially important, since the dye-bath has to be kept at a more or less constant temperature of 113–131°F (45–55°C) throughout the whole process.

Room for dyeing in a 'cold-bath' (cotton, linen etc.)

Vegetable fibres have to be dyed at a relatively low temperature, 68–86°F (20–30°C). In the first part of this book a number of 'classic' methods of dyeing using a cold-bath were described. Mostly these envisaged vats placed in deep, cemented holes or tanks, to allow the cold of the ground to provide the correct temperature. This old, universally used method may well be justified for those producing resist-patterned cloth (e.g. blue-print) on a larger scale, but for those whose undertakings are more modest, the modifications suggested on page 149 in the section on paste-resists may well be more suitable. The dyeing premise should, if it is at all possible, also have a drying room equipped according to the process of dyeing employed.

Tools and equipment

A graduated jug of stainless steel, litre size or larger

Glass measure, 4–11 fl oz (100–300 ml), for measuring the stock solution and liquid chemicals

Glass rods

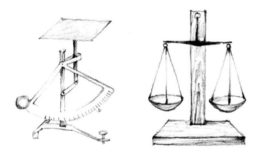

Weighing scale, letter-weight or laboratory balance for more exact measurements

Weights for the above

Test paper see page 126

Glass balls about $\frac{3}{4}''$ (2 cm) diameter for raising the level of the stock solution in its container. See page 122

Large scales kitchen or similar, for weighing cloth, yarn and larger quantities of chemicals

Measuring spoons

Porcelain mortar, plus pestle, for crushing pieces of natural indigo etc.

Spoons of stainless steel for measuring out powdery substances

Funnel, plastic or stainless steel

Glass jars with screw-tops (plastic or bakelite) for storing stock solution

Rubber gloves

Labels, sticky, for putting on the storage jars

Labels, tie-on, for notes and identifying dyed material

Cotton twine for tying hanks of yarn before wetting down and dyeing

Dyeing buckets, preferably made of stainless steel, for 5–50 quarts (5 l–50 l) depending on your needs

Upright tank of stainless steel or plastic, for blue-print etc. that has to be lowered into the bath flat. See page 156.

Tubs, pails of stainless steel or plastic for rinsing and washing; possibly for dyeing

Rods, wooden rounds, $1\frac{1}{4}''–1\frac{1}{2}''$ (3–4 cm) thick and some 32" (80 cm) long, without knots and well cleaned. Some that are un-dyed or only slightly coloured should be kept for using with light colours

Cling film to keep the air from reaching the surface of the liquid, if the dyeing process has to be interrupted

Thermometer graduated 32–212°F (0–100°C)

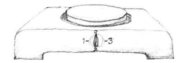

Stove, preferably one which allows the heat to be regulated

Drying frame of strong wooden rods (about 7' or 2 m long) and high trestles for drying hanks of yarn

Electric fan, a small hand-held fan for drying test-dyes and a larger, preferably wall-fan for drying yarn and cloth in the drying room

Blue-print and batik require a few special materials in addition to those listed above. These are described in the section on resist-pastes, pages 150 and 154.

BLUE-PRINT

Paste-resist Today

'The blocks for printing on linen were cut out of pear-wood. They were dipped in a white substance which was continually made smooth, like a thin gruel; after the block had been dipped in this and pressed on the linen, fine white sand was sprinkled on the wet design to which it stuck; this substance repulsed the dye when the cloth was lowered into the bath to be dyed, so that the printed design remained white, without colour, after the whole was dyed.'

Carl Linnaeus: *Travels in West Gotland*, 1746

For all its brevity, the above description of blue-printing at a dye-works in southern Sweden gives one a good comprehensive picture of the technique, as it was practised in Sweden two hundred years and more ago.

In the first part of this book a number of different resists and related dyeing processes have been described. They have been taken from different textile cultures and clearly illustrate the variety of form that is possible. Nor does the older literature advance any one or more methods as being the only and absolutely best. On the contrary, the old instruction books give all sorts of recipes for pastes of varying composition and a number of alternatives for indigo-baths. The number of recipes can be regarded as evidence of the technical difficulties encountered, as well as showing how many possibilities were available for achieving the desired result.

It would be impossible and wrong to say how many recipes for blue-print pastes and baths could be guaranteed to succeed. Instead, I have preferred to give a summary of the ingredients and qualities of the different resist-pastes, as well as to suggest various compositions of pastes, plus a few examples of suitable indigo-baths. Those who wish to work with some form of indigo-resist ought to remember that the instructions are to be regarded, above all, as rudimentary but typical examples of blue-print, on the basis of which each must himself experiment to achieve the methods best suited to his own requirements and wishes.

Cloth to be patterned by resist and dyed with indigo should be drip-dried before being given the final treatment. The picture on the left shows Josef Koó inspecting the day's product (a cloth with sample designs) on the dyeing-ground outside his dye-works.

147

The Composition of Pastes

A resist can be composed in various ways depending on the demands made on the result, which can vary from uncomplicated clay-paste, via the complex 'chemical' pastes of Central Europe to the Asiatic 'mechanical' mixtures of resin and wax. In the section 'White design – blue background', on page 44, the different types are described. Below follows a list of groups of substances from which the ingredients of a paste are usually chosen:

Thickening Flour (rice, soya, wheat etc.), starch (dextrin), gum (gum arabic etc.)

Fillings Insoluble materials that act as a mechanical protection during dyeing; of these the most important are kaolin (china clay) and fine sand.

Substantives that form a protective layer Substances with a chemical action that form impenetrable sediments in the alkaline indigo-bath. Among these are cuprous salts (blue vitriol, verdigris, nitrate of copper), aluminium salts (usually alum – cheap but not very effective, aluminium sulphate – more expensive, but better – and acetate of lead).

Substantives that form protective layers Substances whose action is mechanical, which, having congealed, hamper the dye-solution from penetrating the fibres. First among these is resin (*Resina colofonium*) and ordinary beeswax, rich clays (blue clay) and tallow.

Substantives that provide consistency such as fat, lard and fatty oils. These are used to make the paste more malleable and easier to apply.

Drying-inhibitants aimed at preventing cracking in the protective layer when the atmosphere is extremely dry. First and foremost: glycerine.

Blocks and templates used to print with rice- or kaolin-paste must be carefully washed immediately after use, since pieces of paste left behind can later be almost impossible to remove.

PRINTING WITH PASTE

The material for blue-printing is almost without exception cotton and thus has to be free from finishings, vegetable wax etc. It is best bought from shops which sell materials for batik-work and dyeing.

The material is placed on a printing table, with a rubber-cloth and some suitably soft underlay (foam rubber or felt). The edges are fixed down with masking tape to prevent slipping during printing. The main dimensions of the pattern are marked out with pencil.

The paste is applied with blocks made of wood, linoleum, metal or with a template of nylon gauze. The Japanese often sprinkle the paste on using a forcing-bag with a fine copper nozzle.

To ensure that the raised parts of the stamp get the right amount of paste, a 'block-pad' should be used, onto which the paste has been brushed (or scraped) evenly and to a suitable thickness. The pad consists of a layer of plastic, a piece of foam rubber and a piece of plywood underneath. Immediately after printing is finished – or has been interrupted – the blocks and templates must be scrupulously cleaned with tepid water and a soft brush. Before putting the block onto the actual material it should be tested on a piece of paper or odd piece of material. After the impression, the paste (chemical paste containing various metallic salts) has to dry, that is to say harden, for some weeks, often a month. The longer it is allowed to dry, the better it will stand up to the dye-bath. A clay paste needs only a few days in which to dry before it can be used for dyeing. Rice-paste can dry in an airing cupboard and be used almost at once. If the paste contains copper salts it may be advantageous to allow a longer time for drying. Wax-resin resist can be used as soon as the layer has hardened properly.

Recipe for kaolin paste

Kaolin	2 oz (60 g)
Water	2 fl oz (60 ml)
Gum arabic 1:1	8 tsp (40 g)
Water for dissolving	1½ fl oz (40 ml)
Blue vitriol	8 tsp (40 g)
Copper acetate	4 tsp (20 g)
Tartaric acid or vinegar	1 tbsp (15 ml)
Tallow	2–4 tsp (10–20 g)
Olive oil	1 tsp (6 ml)
Alum (after cooling)	4 tsp (20 g)
Water for diluting	1½–2 fl oz (40–60 ml)

Preparation of the paste

The paste should be prepared in a vessel that will tolerate heat (e.g. stainless steel). The process begins by stirring the kaolin into the boiling water, using glass rods that are absolutely clean. The gum solution is added next and carefully stirred in. Then the copper salts and tartaric acid are mixed in and the melted tallow, oil (corn or olive) added.

The pot with the paste is then heated for half an hour in a bath of boiling water, being stirred now and again. Its consistency should now be that of a thick gruel. Water that may have evaporated is replaced, if necessary.

As soon as the mixture has cooled, the alum can be added, after which the paste is transferred to a glass jar with a close-fitting lid. Label the jar to show its contents. Allow the paste to stand for several days before using it. Provided the lid is more or less airtight and there is not much air space above the paste, the latter will keep for years.

Variants of paste

The recipe above is only one of countless others that were in use a hundred or more years ago. Other variants and the personal experience of those who try them may well lead to yet other and perhaps better pastes.

One effective substance that can be added is lead acetate, but because it is poisonous this must be handled with extreme care. For a quantity similar to that given above the most suitable amount of lead acetate would be 1 oz (20–25 g) dissolved in 1½ fl oz (20 ml) of water.

Pastes with kaolin and tallow (fat)

German blue-printers working in Pennsylvania, USA, at the end of the 18th century and in the early 19th century, used pastes composed of kaolin, gum arabic and tallow (fat). Printed material now in the Pennsylvania Farm Museum, in Landis Valley, shows that this was a satisfactory combination.

In France and England, towards the end of the 18th century, a special form of resist-print, the so-called Kasimir-print, was being produced. Ingenious machines were used to apply the paste mechanically. The paste consisted of equal parts of 'Russian' tallow and kaolin which were heated to make what the old instruction books call a 'creamy' consistency. The resist gradually hardened and allowed the cloth to be worked and dyed with indigo.

Pastes of clay

The oldest forms of resist-dyeing probably employed a variety of clays. One suitable clay is ordinary blue clay mixed with water to such a consistency that it can be printed or pressed onto the cloth. After drying, which should not be so vigorous that the paste cracks, it provides a short-term guard against an indigo solution of moderate strength.

The covering power of clay paste can be increased by adding alum (about 10 g to 100 g of paste). The clay should be as pure as possible, i.e. free of particles of vegetable matter and earth.

Tallow and tallow-resin resist

Tallow comes in varying consistencies. To be suitable as a resist, it should be firm and hard. Soft and gluey tallow (like lard) gives poor protection and runs easily into the material fibres during printing.

Before the tallow can be used, it must be melted in a small saucepan and then strained to remove impurities and solids. The purified tallow is then poured into a shallow aluminium dish, the bottom part of which is covered with a piece of felt (foam rubber should not be used). The piece of felt should be soaked, but the level of the tallow must not be above it. The dish should be kept warm the whole time on the lowest heat of an electric plate.

The block is pressed lightly against the blanket and then quickly placed in the desired position on the cloth. This process is repeated until the whole surface of the cloth has received its due number of prints. After being printed, the cloth should hang for some days to allow the tallow to harden properly.

An indigo vat for cotton should be maintained at a temperature of 68–75°F (20–24°C). This comparatively low temperature has the effect that the tallow resist, especially if the quality is high, protects against a fairly saturated, dark blue vat. Thus the following strength is recommended:

Block-pad for paste-resist printing (see page 149).

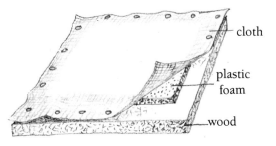

cloth

plastic foam

wood

Bright bath	5 quarts	10 quarts
	(5 litres)	(10 litres)
Stock solution of vat	2 fl oz	3½ fl oz
colour	(50 ml)	(100 ml)

See also pages 130–2.

A good tallow, which hardens well after the printing, seldom needs any extra additives. However, sometimes you may want to strengthen the protective effect. A good product to use is *resin*, which has an exceptional resist ability. Indian dyers and Javanese batik producers have used this product for centuries. The only disadvantage is that it is very difficult to wash it away from the material after the dyeing. You should therefore only add small amounts to the tallow paste e.g.

Melted (and purified)		
tallow	3½ fl oz	100 ml
Resin (pulverised)	4 tsp	4 g

Recipe for rice-paste (lead free)

Rice-flour	1½ oz	3 oz
	(50 g)	(100 g)
Water at 86°F	7 fl oz	14 fl oz
(30°C)	(200 ml)	(400 ml)
Blue vitriol	½ oz	1 oz
	(15 g)	(30 g)
Verdigris	½ oz	1 oz
	(15 g)	(30 g)
Tartaric acid	⅛ oz (2 tsp)	¼ oz (4 tsp)
(vinegar)	(2 g, 10 ml)	(4 g, 20 ml)
Alum	½ oz	1 oz
	(15 g)	(30 g)
Olive oil	1–2 tsp	2–4 tsp
	(5–10 ml)	(10–20 ml)

Preparation of the paste

Mix the rice-flour with water, a little at a time, in a vessel of glass or stainless steel.

Heat it up to a temperature of 194–212°F (90–100°C) in a water-bath for 4–6 hours, stirring now and again. The paste will become considerably thicker; evaporated water should be replaced.

When the paste has acquired a smooth, pliable consistency, the blue vitriol, verdigris and tartaric acid (vinegar) should be carefully stirred in. Now, cover the paste well with a good lid or foil and put to cool overnight. Once it is cool, the alum is added and the paste left to stand for one or two hours before being used. If the paste becomes too thick it can be carefully thinned with water. However, take care that it does not become too liquid.

The paste can be applied with wooden blocks, templates or by brush. A lime-sulphate bath is to be preferred, but if its alkalinity is kept very low, it will resist even a hydrogen sulphite bath. A paste containing metallic salts should as a rule be hardened for a few weeks after printing but a rice

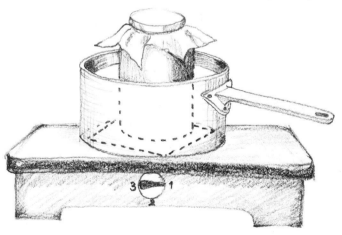

Water-bath for rice-paste.

The basic outline of the design is drawn in with a lead pencil thus providing a guide for placing the blocks.

The printing-block with paste on it being placed on the cloth using the guide-lines.

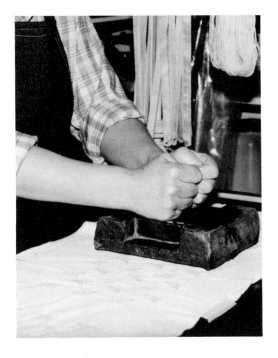

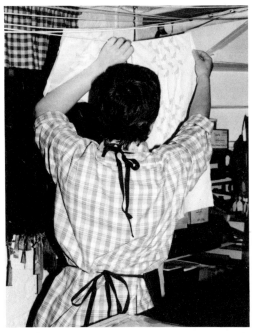

A few strong blows on the block make the paste attach to the cloth properly.

The printed cloth is hung up to dry and harden.

paste can be quickly dried in a cupboard.
Note   As soon as you have finished printing, carefully wash the templates and blocks in lukewarm water. Sample prints should be done on paper or spare material similar to the one to be used later.

Wax-resin resist

In many parts of Asia resist mixtures of beeswax and resin have long been used. They are applied to the cloth by brush or with printing blocks.

Beeswax by itself is too flimsy and sensitive to alkali to resist an indigo solution on its own. Resin, a byproduct of the manufacture of wood turpentine, mixes with wax to produce a combination that is both strong and easy to work.

Recipe for wax-resin resist

	normal resist	strong resist
Beeswax	3 oz (100 g)	3 oz (100 g)
Resin	½–2 tsp (5–10 g)	3–4 tsp (15–20 g)

Preparation of a resist mixture

The mixture of wax and resin is heated in a flat, wide dish in which is a piece of blanket, against which the block will be pressed and then swiftly applied to the cloth. Foam rub-

ber cannot be used at temperatures above 212°F (100°C).

It is important to maintain the resist mixture at an even temperature throughout the process. The temperature is adjusted both to the texture of the cloth and the tem-

perature of the workroom. Thus a 392°F (200°C) thermometer should always be put in the dish. For thin weave and a hot workroom about 212–248°F (100–120°C) may be enough, while a coarse weave and a cool workroom call for 232°F or 130°C or so more. The mixture should never be allowed to reach 302–320°F (150–160°C), for then there will be a danger of the resist being burned and of the mixture catching fire. If that last should happen, remember:

Keep calm !
Smother the flames!
Never use water !

The blocks can be made of metal (copper or brass) like the Javanese ones. Ordinary wooden blocks can be used perfectly well, as is done in India and neighbouring countries, but they should not be given too detailed or close a pattern. The simplest instrument for printing can be made from

pieces of bamboo of varying thicknesses, which can be used individually or combined to make a matrix.

A wax-resin resist has considerable strength to resist different indigo solutions and so even a hydrosulphite solution can be used. Repeated dipping to obtain a deep-blue colour will not, as a rule, harm the resist.

Removal of the resist after dyeing requires first pressing out the mixture with a hot iron between a couple of newspapers (not new ones!). Then the material is worked in acetone for a while, after which the remaining pieces of the resin will wash out in a bath with some suitable washing-material.

Old Indian printing blocks cut in rounds of some hard wood. The two top ones are intended for printing a thickened iron solution that will produce the black outline of the design on the cloth. Area of the larger: 8″ × 9″ (20 × 22 cm).

BLUE-PRINT DYEING

Lime-vitriol bath for blue-print

The lime-vitriol bath has been known since the middle of the 18th century, since when it has been used principally in conjunction with resist-dyeing for blue-print. The reducing agent used is green vitriol and lime. The proportion of the ingredients can vary quite considerably, but it is always better not to use too little. For blue-print with a chemical paste, a vitriol-lime bath is decidedly preferable to the hydrogen sulphite bath, which has a tendency to dissolve the relatively sensitive paste layer.

The water in the bath had best be soft water, that is either rain water or melted snow (though not new fallen snow which can be polluted with industrial outfall). If using tap water, do not let it gush out but leave it to stand so that the oxygen can disperse.

For dyeing, one should use deep, narrow dye-tanks into which the printed material can be lowered flat. There should, too, be enough space beneath the cloth in the tank (4″–8″ or 10–20 cm) to allow the sediment to collect. For test dyeing and dyeing smaller pieces you can use a tank of stainless steel like that pictured on page 156, which holds 8–10 qt or 8–10 litres of solution. It is important that the tank can be covered after, and between, dyeings with a close-fitting lid or plastic film. The solution should not be allowed to grow too cold in winter. For dyeing, 68–75°F (20–24°C) is the best temperature.

Stainless steel tank for dyeing blue-print.

When using a vitriol-lime bath and similar solutions it is important that there should be plenty of room at the bottom of the tank for sediment.

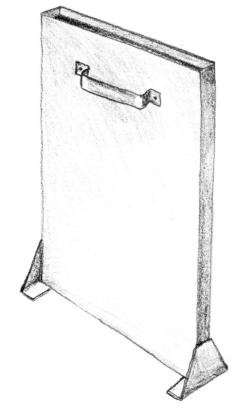

156

Recipe for green vitriol-lime bath

A. Stock solution (intended for *c.* 8 quarts or 8 litres bath)

1. Indigo — 2 tsp (10 g)
   water at 140°F
   (60°C) — 3½ fl oz (100 ml)
2. Burnt lime (cal-
   cium oxide) — 8 tsp (40 g)
   Water at 77°F
   (25°C) — 3½ fl oz (100 ml)
   Water at 140°F
   (60°C) — 11 fl oz (300 ml)
3. Green   vitriol
   (fresh) — 8 tsp (40 g)
   Water at 140°F
   (60°C) — 14 fl oz (400 ml)

1. The *indigo* is stirred into 3½ fl oz (100 ml) of water at 140°F (60°C).
2. The *burnt lime* is slaked with 3½ fl oz (100 ml) of water at 77°F (25°C). *NB* This generates considerable heat! Then it is diluted with 9 fl oz (300 ml) of water at 140°F (60°C); if using slaked lime (calcium hydroxide) this calls for about a third more of water.
3. The *green vitriol* (fresh) is dissolved in 14 fl oz (400 ml) of water at 140°F (60°C).

Solutions 1 and 2 are put together in a stainless steel vessel of about 2 quarts (2 litres) and then No. 3 solution (green vitriol) is added and the whole covered with a lid or plastic film. This stock solution is then kept at 122–140°F (50–60°C) in a water-bath for 4–6 hours or overnight. It should be carefully stirred now and then, the covering being replaced on each occasion.

B. Blank bath
   Water at 68–75°F — about 6 quarts
   (20–24°C) — about 7000 ml
1. Burnt lime — 2 tsp (10 g)
   Water at 95°F — 5 fl oz
   (35°C) — (150 ml)
2. Green vitriol (fresh) — 2 tsp (10 g)
   Water at about 140°F — 5 fl oz
   (60°C) — (150 ml)

Before the stock solution is added to it, the blank bath must be sharpened with small quantities of lime and green vitriol.

1. The lime is slaked with 5 fl oz (150 ml) of water. (*NB* Remember heat is generated!)
2. The green vitriol is dissolved in 5 fl oz (150 ml) of water.
   The two solutions are added to the blank bath which is then left to stand for a couple of hours, before the stock solution is put into the bath.

C. *Preparation of the dye-bath*
Carefully pour the stock solution into the blank bath. Stir and allow the bath to stand for a couple of hours, or overnight in the case of a largish bath. It has to be well covered with a lid or foil. Its temperature should be about 68–75°F (20–24°C).

Instructions for dyeing with a vitriol-lime bath

Before dyeing begins check that the bath is in order. The solution should be yellow or yellow-green in colour, which indicates that reduction has been completed and that the indigo dye-stuff has dissolved. The scum (bloom) that forms on the surface and which is a sure sign that everything is functioning well, is removed, but is saved and poured back into the bath when dyeing is over or when the next bath is being prepared.

The material to be dyed is fixed to hooks (or clips) in a wooden or metal rod which can lie across the top of the dye-vat. Larger baths require a 'ring-frame' which can be lowered into the bath, as shown in the illustration on page 54. It is an advantage if the lower edges of the material can be weighted, e.g. by fixing on lead net sinkers or something similar.

Cloth must be put into the bath dry and should be held quite still during the 10–15 minutes that dyeing normally takes. After a dipping period of 20–30 minutes the shade cannot be deepened. As with other indigo-dyeing, here, too, when it is desired to achieve deeper shades, it is best (if the paste will stand up to it) to undertake several dips instead. Between each dip into the bath, complete oxidisation of the dye must be allowed to take place, that is to say, it must be in the air for at least 10–20 minutes.

Sharpening of the bath

The dye-bath must always have a yellow or slightly yellow-green shade. If, in the course of dyeing it becomes more a pure green, it will have to be sharpened with green vitriol. The quantity to be used is decided by how green the solution has become. One can begin by adding $\frac{1}{4}$ tsp per quart (1 g per litre) of solution, then let the bath stand for a while. If it still does not look normal, add more vitriol. If the solution turns dark brownish, there is too little lime in it and in that case it has to be sharpened with about $\frac{1}{4}$ tsp per quart (1.5 g per litre) in the bath. When the dyed material is lifted out of the bath, it should have a yellow-brown (beige) colour which gradually turns dark green and ends up dark blue. If the cloth is light green when it is lifted out, this is a warning that the indigo has been used up and fresh stock solution will have to be added. If stirring produces no 'bloom', both iron and lime will have to be added, $\frac{1}{4}$ tsp per quart (1 g per litre) of the former and $\frac{1}{4}$ tsp per quart (1.5 g per litre) of the latter.

If dyeing has to be interrupted, the bath must be covered over with plastic cloth. Before each dyeing the solution in the bath must be stirred, after which, once all solid particles have sunk to the bottom, dyeing can be resumed.

After-treatment

Freshly dyed material must be drip-dried before anything more is done to it. This will produce clearer designs and a darker shade of blue. As soon as the cloth has dried, it must be treated with a souring bath: a bath of water to which acetic acid has been added until it has a definitely acid taste. This neutralises the lime in the fabric, dissolves the paste and enhances the whiteness of the design. Those who are accustomed to dealing with sulphuric acid can use that instead (but see page 133).

The dye can also be hardened by allowing the cloth to lie for 15–30 minutes in the water-bath to which a fine washing-agent has been added at a temperature of about 176–194°F (80–90°C). (See pastes on page 149.) Several thorough rinsings and washings conclude the dyeing process.

Detail of a silk fabric from Nepal patterned with a wax-resin resist. Dyed indigo on a yellow background.

DESIGNS FOR BLUE-PRINT

The resist-pastes used in making blue-print can be applied to the cloth with wood-blocks, templates or with a brush. There is no difficulty in making the paste itself of such a consistency that it suits the intended form of application. It is easy either to thicken or to thin it. But whatever you choose, woodblock or template, you must have regard to the shape of the design. Because the paste has limited power of resistance to the dissolving action of the dye-bath, all larger surfaces tend to suffer damage quite soon after the material has been lowered into the bath. This results in the dye seeping through and forming trails of colour that can spoil the effect. This limitation has led to blue-print designs being given a special form. The ideal is a design of nothing but dots or dots in conjunction with narrow lines. Study of blue-print work

from different parts of the world has shown how these limitations have created a characteristic micro-form of design.

It is easy to make your own woodblock suitable for blue-print. Metal pins or small nails are hammered into a flat piece of wood in some required pattern (see page 160). On the other side of the piece of wood you fix a little handle. It is desirable to treat your block with varnish or oil to prevent it being harmed when paste is washed off at the end of dyeing.

You should beware of old print-blocks that one sometimes comes across. If you like the design, it is a good idea to make a copy in some plastic material. Then you have a good matrix which will stand up to quite rough treatment.

Printing block from northern Hälsingland, in Sweden, the design on which has been made by driving in metal pins.

Blue-print made with the block on the opposite page, using kaolin paste and a hydrogen sulphite bath.

When a building in Norway was pulled down some years ago, some thirty printing-blocks and a club used in the printing process were discovered. The building had previously belonged to the Lampe family, which had been in business there, as dyers and fabric printers, since 1798. The blocks were found under some floor-boards and behind wainscotting presumably installed when alterations were made at the beginning of the 19th century. They are now in the Historical Museum in Bergen.

The designs opposite (and on the following pages) come from this collection and were drawn by Bente Merete Hansen. The elegantly varied and modelled Mir-i-bota motif was probably intended for the corner of a cloth or kerchief. It shows great similarities with Indian and Persian designs. The design on the next page is a typical border and of no great quality.

Blocks made on the Continent were from the beginning normally made of walnut, later of pear, and were cut in one piece. In Sweden and Norway it was usual to use birch. The design plate itself was cut from a round of hard wood and this made it possible to include considerable detail. Often blocks were made of several layers, with the direction of the wood's fibres laid transversely, before being joined with glue or wooden dowels. From the end of the seventeenth century metal pins were used for finer detail, and so gradually their use was extended until pretty well the whole design was reproduced in pins and metal strips.

A printing-block can be used for different kinds of print, for oil-based pigments as well as for white-resist blue-print pastes. The shape and above all the size and density of the parts of the design usually decide the degree of suitability. But a block intended for printing a pigment with relatively large pattern-surfaces can very easily be used for resist-print, if a paste containing a wax-resin mixture is chosen. Many of the oil blocks from Lampe's printing-shop were probably originally intended for some form of direct-print, but later used for the far more popular blue-print.

Designs from printing blocks in which all the details are produced with thin metal strips and pins. The block comes from Skofia Loka in Slovenia and has probably been used in the dye-works there, the buildings of which are still preserved. The picture on the left shows the design printed as white-resist (see the impression on page 168).

Design from a printing-block cut of one whole piece of wood from Västerbotten in Sweden. Full scale.

Impression from a block with metal strips and pins from Skofia Loka in Slovenia. Its measurements are $6\frac{1}{2}'' \times 8''$ (17×20 cm).

Impression from a block, cut from one whole piece of wood, from Hälsingland, Sweden. Its measurements are $6\frac{1}{2}'' \times 9''$ (17×23 cm).

169

TO GET A BLUE DYE OF INDIGO

—with which you can dye blue
wool, linen and cotton.
from: *An honest and reliable dye-book*, 1759

Take a wooden vessel large enough for 8 jugs of water; then take a copper-kettle, into this pour 7 jugs of water and 8 weights of coarse madder, a stoup of bran, 1 pound of grey potash, allow the kettle to come to the boil and let it boil for a quarter of an hour, then pour it into the firkin in which the dye shall be, lay something over it so that it keeps warm; take 4 weights of *Indigo* in a small pot with a quarter of a gallon of water, 4 weights of potash, allow it to boil for half an hour, while it is boiling pound gently on the bottom of the pan with a pestle so that the indigo becomes as fine as powder, when it is boiled, take the pan off the fire and allow it to cool somewhat, and also pound evenly so that the indigo becomes truly small, then pour from the firkin what is clear and with the pestle pound the thickness on the bottom of the pan until it becomes quite fine: then pour all into the firkin and rinse the pan clean, and stir well the content of the firkin and allow it to stand 12 hours, then stir it again, and so continue until 24 hours have passed, then the dye is ready to dye. *NB* All woollen yarn that is to be dyed blue must first be washed in warm water and dyed wet. But linen yarn is dyed dry. All cotton yarn is boiled for half an hour in pure water and dyed wet.

1 jug	=	2.6 litres
1 weight	=	13.3 g
1 stoup	=	1.3 litres
1 pound	=	425 g
1 bucket	=	49 litres

Til at fättja en blå färg af *Indi-go* ſom man kan färga blådt både Ylle, Linne och Bom-ull, nemligen:

Man tager et trä = käril, af 8 kan-nor watns ſtorlek, ſå tager man en Koppar = kettel, ther uti ſlår man 7 kannor watn och 8 lod grof krapp, et ſtop Hwete=kli, 1 ſkålpund grå påt-aſka, låter ketteln komma at koka, låt thet koka uti en fierdedels tima , ſlå thet ſedan uti byttan ſom färgen ſkal wara uti, lägg något therpå, at thet håller ſig warmt, tag ſå 4 Lod Indigo uti en liten Gryta med et ſtop watn, 4 Lod Potaſka, låt thet koka i en half tima, medan thet kokar, ſtöter man med en ſtötel ganſka ſakta på Gryt-botn at Indigon blifwer helt ſin ſom Puder, når thet är koft, tager man Grytan af elden och låter litet kall-

na, ſamt ſtöter jemt at Indigon blif-wer wål ſmå, ſedan håller man uti byttan thet klara och rifwer med ſtö-telen thet tiocka på bottnen i Grytan til theß thet blifwer helt fint: tå ſlår man alt uti byttan och ſköljer Grytan ren, och rör wål om i byttan och låter then ſtå uti 12 timar, ſedan rörer man färgen om igen och låter ſtå i 2 tim-mar, ſedan 2 timar äro förbi, rörer man om igen, ock ſå fortfar man til 24 timar äro förbi; tå är färgen fär-dig at färga.

NB. Alt Ullgarn ſom ſkal färgas blådt, måſte förſt twättas uti warmt watn och ſå wått färgas. Men Lingarnet färgas tort. All Bomullsgarn kokas en half tima i rent watn och färgas wått.

Will man nu färga Ullgarn eller Tyg grönt, ſå ſkal man färgat gult förſt, och ſedan i ſamma blå färgen med thet gula ſå blifwer thet grönt.

URINE BATH ACCORDING TO CAJSA WARG, 1762

To dye wool blue

'Take urine, preferably of those who drink strong drinks, put it into a firkin, or jug that has a lid with cloth between, so that it is kept well stopped, and allow it to stand in a warm, but not hot oven, for 3 to 4 days; then the clear is poured off, but the thick is thrown away and the firkin is rinsed clean, then the clear is poured back in. The indigo is pounded quite fine in a . . . bag made of thin linen . . . which is placed in the clear urine, where it is left for 4 to 5 days, but rubbed once a day, after which a bit of woollen yarn is put in to test the colour. If the wool is green when it has lain there half a day, the dye is good: then, first, each skein is dipped in it, the one after the other, and wrung out; then they are all thoroughly shaken out and laid quite flat in the firkin. When they have lain there from morning until noon, they are again wrung out and put back again as they were after being thoroughly shaken out. Thus they must lie 2 or 3 days, till they become as dark as is wanted, then the dye is wrung out of it . . . the yarn is then washed and then rinsed . . . then it can be hung up and dried.'

The proportions for this dye are for one mark of woollen yarn (about 425 g) one weight (1313 g) indigo, if it is to be dark, and of urine as much as will stand well above the yarn, otherwise it will become speckled, likewise if the firkin is not kept well closed, and see to it that the dye always simmers tepid, but not hotter.

Comment

The rather vague indications for temperature given at the beginning and end of the recipe should be understood as 86°–104°F (30–40°C).

The advice that the yarn should be 'wrung out' should not be taken; instead, the solution should be squeezed out of the yarn so as to avoid felting of the fibres.

The recipe gives no indication of how old the urine should be, but other books say it should be about half a year. The yarn will lose the smell after being aired for some time.

Mill for grinding indigo, taken from *Lexicon der Farben-Technik*, Vienna 1903.

BLUE ON WOOL
(hot bath)

from: Johan Östberg's *Färgbok* of 1833

Pour urine which should preferably be half a year old into a stone pitcher or oaken-cask of 8 jugs (about 20 litres) in which salt has never been put. Soak finely powdered indigo (about 20 g) in water for 14 days, sieve it through a fine sieve into an oaken vessel, and pour it into a vat. Make it as hot as your hand will endure and stir it industriously. Pour it back into the same vessel as soon as it has become sufficiently warm, and the yarn then placed in it for a longer or shorter time, according to whether it shall be lighter or darker, and now and again working it industriously. Then take it out and rinse it in urine, the urine is poured back into the dye and the yarn immediately rinsed in pure water.

Blue-print blocks from Steinberg in Austria.
The design is composed with brass pins and thin metal strips.

HOW A COLD BATH IS SET

(cold bath)

from: Carl Hedman's *Ny och fullstandig fargbok* of 1847
(New and complete dye-book)

A large wooden barrel of 10 buckets (about 500 litres) capacity is filled with cold water.

A pound (425 g) fine indigo, well ground with water, four pounds (1700 g) green vitriol, melted in hot water, four pounds (1700 g) unslaked lime are mixed together in a vat with two or three pails of water and then brought to the boil while being industriously stirred with a stick. When it has cooled pour it into the barrel and stir. It must stand for two hours so that it can clear, after which the bath is ready.

Block from north Hälsingland.

SUPPLIERS

Great Britain

Matheson's Dyes and Chemicals
Marcon Place
London E.8 01–254–9684

Williams Ltd.
Greville House
Hibernia Road
Hounslow, Mddx. TW3 01–570–7766

United States

Brooks & Flynn
Box 5009
Petaluma, CA 94953
800–822–2372
In California: 800–345–2026

Cerulean Blue Ltd.
P.O. Box 21168
Seattle, WA 98111
206–443–7744

Dharma Trading o.
Box 916
San Rafael, CA 94915
In California: 415–456–7657

Earth Guild
1 Tingle Alley
Asheville, NC 28801
704–255–7818

PRO Chemical & Dye Inc.
P.O. Box 14
Somerset, MA 02726
617–676–3838

Rupert, Gibbon & Spider
718 College St.
Healdsburg, CA 95448
707–433–9577

Textile Resources
P.O. Box 90245
Long Beach, CA 90809
213–431–9611

For *Fabrics*:

Testfabrics Inc.
P.O. Drawer "O"
Middlesex, NJ 08846
201–469–6446

Material for indigo-dyeing from Nigeria in West
Africa.
    The picture shows balls of indigo (*elu*), parts
of some unidentified plant which used to be put
in the solution and comes from Abeokuta, also
lime and wood-ash from the dyers' town, Kano.

PEOPLE AND PLACES

Brief particulars of some of the people and places mentioned in the book.

Cajsa Warg (1703–1769), authoress of a famous work *Hjälpreda uti Hushållningen för unga Fruentimber (Housekeeping Guide for Young Women)*, which became the second most printed book in Sweden after the Bible. Already in the first edition of 1755 there were a number of excellent recipes for dyeing, and after the tenth edition it was enlarged with a 'Dyeing Book' containing 175 recipes. The instructions show unusual expertise for that time, and the linguistic account shows a pleasant clarity.

Colbert, Jean Baptiste (1619–1683) Louis XIV's finance minister who had the task of restoring France's collapsed economy. His interests extended beyond financial matters to science, cultural affairs and the arts. In 1669 he introduced a law (*Ars tinctoria fundamentalis*) which, among other things, regulated the use of textile dyes. It re-established the dyers guild, so-called 'fine dyers', who after this were the only ones who might use the best dyes such as indigo, woad, madder and cochineal, while the so-called inferior dyers had to use litmus, saffron, dye-woods and orleans. As a person, Colbert was serious, keen and of a slightly cold nature, which made the authoress Marie de Sévigné call him 'the North'.

Pliny, Gaius, the Elder (AD 23) Roman official and scholar with a burning interest in science and research. His *Historia Naturalis*, of which some 200 manuscript copies have survived, is a sort of encyclopaedia of the natural sciences, cultural history and technical matters. The contents of the 27 volumes are based on more than two thousand works by more than a hundred authors and despite an approach at times somewhat fanciful it is a priceless source of information about the world of antiquity. Pliny's death was like his life. During the eruption of Vesuvius in AD 79 his thirst for knowledge led him to investigate it at close quarters and in doing so he was killed by the sulphur fumes.

Marco Polo (born about 1254 in Venice, died about 1325) Italian explorer who has given us the most remarkable descriptions of travels in the history of exploration. While a prisoner-of-war in the war between Venice and Genoa he dictated his experiences in Central Asia and China under the Mongol dynasty.

Xun Zi (Hsün Tzu) Confucian philosopher, probably born about 312 BC. The quotation at the beginning of the chapter on the indigo-plant introduces one of his essays which has the title *Quan Xue*, encouragement to study.

Fuchs, Leonhard (1501–1566) German physician and botanist. One of the foremost of those who broke new ground in medicine and botany in the 16th century. The picture on page 25 is from his *Läbliche Abbildung und Contrafaytung aller Kreüter*, published in Basle in 1545. The plant family Fuchsia is named after him.

Runge, Ferdinand (1795–1867) German chemist. Responsible for the fundamental investigation of coal tar which led to the discovery of aniline, phenol and pyrrol, which were to have such great theoretical and practical significance. He was also the first to succeed in producing dye derivatives of aniline (the word aniline comes from the Arabic word for indigo = *anil*). The author of a number of exemplary chemical practices and papers.

Hofmann, August Wilhelm (1818–1892) In 1845 was given the post of director of the new Royal College of Chemistry in London, where he worked for twenty years or so, and where during the 1800s he prepared the scientific foundations of the chemistry of organic dyes. His *Introduction to Modern Chemistry* is an exceptionally good textbook. His contemporaries called him an excellent speaker and a great personality.

Macquer, Joseph Pierre and *Hellot, Jean* Up to the end of the 17th century the process of dyeing was based on purely empirical knowledge. The start of the 18th century saw people beginning to look for more scientific explanations and interesting themselves in the chemical and mechanical processes of dyeing. A couple of important books paved the way for this new approach: first was Hellot's *Théorie chemique de la Teinture des Étoffes* published in 1740, in which he deals with indigo at length. This was followed in 1750 by his great work *L'Art de la Teinture*. Then, in 1763, came a book by Macquer who was particularly interested in the chemistry and methods of silk-dyeing, *L'Art du Teinturier en Soie*. The pictures on pages 36 and 38–9 have been taken from the German translation of it published in 1764.

Thunberg, Carl Peter (1743–1828) Explorer, botanist and one of the many famous disciples of Linnaeus. He was specially interested in the flora of Japan and this earned him the title of the Japanese Linnaeus. His book *Resa uti Europa, Africa, Asia förrättad åren 1770–1779* was translated into many languages and earned him considerable renown.

Rosetti, Giovenni (Dates unknown) Director of the artillery depot in Venice, who studied the art of dyeing in Italy and other countries and, in 1560, published a book entitled *Plictho dell'Arte de Tentori*, which contains among other things the earliest known printed pictures of various dyeing processes. A French translation was published in 1716 as *Le Teinturier Parfait*. The facts taken from his work are from the facsimile of the second edition printed in 1548, which was published in 1969.

Golden Triangle An area, in northern Thailand, of wooded hills and fertile valleys, with irregular limestone formations and green, shimmery watercourses. Some of the most fascinating peoples in the world have settled here, including the Karen, Meo (Hmong), Mien (Yao), Lahu and Akha peoples whose different textiles, jewellery etc. are of considerable artistic merit.

Mohenjo-Daro A place in the province of Sind, in Pakistan, on the Indus river, where the remains of a highly developed civilisation of the Copper Age has been discovered. It is perhaps the most important source of finds of the so-called Indus civilisation, the oldest high civilisation in India (2500 BC). The finds include dyed textiles.

Gösta Sandberg has previously been a master of textile dyeing and colour theory at the Swedish State School of Arts, Crafts and Design. For some years he was also visiting lecturer at Barva in Oblika and Šola za Oblikovanje, Ljubljana. With the support of various scientific institutions he has made a large number of tours of Asia, Africa, Central Europe and the Balkans in order to document disappearing textile dyeing and design techniques.

He has a unique collection of historical dyeing books and textiles with the emphasis on the resist techniques of batik, plangi (tie-and-dye), ikat and blue printing. He has presented his teaching and travel experiences in a number of specialist articles and books.

BIBLIOGRAPHY

Adachi, Barbara, *The living treasures of Japan*, Kodansha International 1973.

Adire Cloth in Nigeria, University of Ibadan 1971.

Adrosko, Rita J., *Natural Dyes and Home Dyeing*, Dower Publication, New York 1971.

Afrika, historiskt panorama, Förlags AB Wiken 1982.

Arkeologiska fynd från Folkrepubliken Kina, Östasiatiska Museet, Stockholm 1974.

Bird, C.L., *The Theory and Practice of Wool Dyeing*, SDC, Bradford 1947.

Bindewald, E., *Bunter Traum auf gewebtem Grund*, Braunschweig 1950.

Bersch, Josef, *Lexikon der Farben-Technik*, Wien 1903.

Bühler, Alfred & Fischer, E., *The Patola of Gujarat*, Basel 1979.

Bühler, Alfred, *Ikat, Batik, Plangi*, Pharos Verlag, Basel 1972.

Chesi, Gert, *De sista afrikanerna*, Kulturhistoriska Förlagen, 1979.

Colour Index, The Society of Dyers and Colourists, Bradford 1971.

Cyrén, Otto, *Syntetiska färgämnen och läkemedel*, Tekniskt folkbibliotek, Stockholm 1939.

Diderot & d'Alembert, *Encyclopédie ou Dictionnaire raisonné des sciences, des arts et des métiers*, Paris 1751.

Dolve, Anders, *Vaid til Blåfarging*, Oslo 1947.

From the Hands of the Hills, Hong Kong 1978.

Fuchs, Leonhard, *Läbliche Abbildung und contrafaytung aller Kreüter,* Basel 1545.

Gadd, Pehr Adrian, *Underrättelse om färgestoften Veides plantering och ans i Finland*, Åbo 1760.

Gardi, René, *Artisans Africains*, Bern 1970.

Geijer, Agnes, *Ur textilkonstens historia*, Lund 1980.

Gelder, Lydia van, *Ikat*, Watson Guptil Publications, New York 1980.

Gittinger, Mattiebelle, *Master-dyers to the World*, Washington 1982.

Gittinger Mattiebelle, *Splendid Symbols*, Washington 1979.

Grunfeld, Frederic, *Wayfares of the Thai Forest* (Acha), Amsterdam 1982.

Grundriss der Färberei und des Zeugdrucks, Vitalis & Dingler, Stuttgart 1839.

Hanak, Elfriede, *Burgenland*, Wien 1978.

Hauge, Victor & Takako, *Folk Traditions in Japanese Art*, Kodansha International, 1978.

Horsfall, R. S. & Lawrie, L. G., *The Dyeing of Textile Fibres*, London 1949.

Hellot, Jean, *L'Art de La Teinture*, Paris 1750.

Henrikson, A. & Hwang Tsu-Yü, *Kinesisk Historia*, Bonniers 1978.

Hermbstädt, S. F., *Magazin für Färber, Zeugdrucker und Bleicher*, Berlin 1804 and 1811.

Indigo rein, BASF, Ludwigshafen 1907.

Indigo Prints of China, Peking 1956.

Izikowitz, K. G., *Lamet hill peasants of French Indochina*, Göteborg 1951.

Izikowitz, K. G., *Över dimmornas berg*, Bonniers 1944.

Jonson, Jonas, *Kina, kyrka, kultur*, Stockholm 1980.

Kinaboken, Natur & Kultur, Stockholm 1982.

Krähenbühl, E. A., *Der zeugdruck*, Basel 1951.

Kunst, Jaap, *Cultural relations between the Balkans and Indonesia*, Amsterdam 1960.

Langewis, Laurens, *Decorative Art in Indonesian Textiles*, Amsterdam 1964.

Larsen, J. L., *The Dyers Art, Ikat, Batik, Plangi*, New York 1976.

Laumann, Maryta M., *The Secret of Excellence in Ancient Chinese Silks*, Taipei 1984.

Lewis, Paul & Elaine, *Peoples of the Golden Triangle*, Stuttgart 1984.

Linden, M. J., *Beyträge für Kottonfabriken und Baumwollenfärberen*, Leipzig 1799.

Lu Pu, *Designs of Chinese Indigo Batik*, Peking 1981.

Lubell, Cecil, *Textile Collections of the World*, New York 1976.

Macquer, P. J., *Die Kunst der Seidenfärberey*, Leipzig 1764.

Marco Polos äventyr i Kina, Rugoff, M. Malmö 1965.

Marco Polos Resor, Forumbiblioteket, 1944.

Miller, Dorothy, *Indigo from seed to dye*, Aptos 1981.

Myrdal, Jan & Kessle, Gun, *Sidenvägen*, Norstedts, Stockholm 1977.

Nakano, Eisha, *Stencil Dyeing*, New York & Tokyo 1982.

Nielsen, Esther, *Farver af Planter*, Borgen, 1983.

Nippon Senshoku-Fu, Toho Shuppansha, Tokyo 1964.

Nippon Colours (Kusaki Zome), Akira Yamazaki, Kamakura 1959.

Oyelola, P, *Nigerian Crafts*, Hong Kong 1981.

Papyrus Graecus Holmiensis, edited by O. Lagercrantz; Uppsala & Leipzig 1913.

Pliny, *Natural History*, vols 1–15, William Heinemann Ltd, London 1952.

Polacoff, Claire, *African Textiles and Dyeing Techniques*, London 1982.

Raffles, Sir Thomas, *History of Java*, London 1817.

Real-Enzyklopädie der Gesamten Pharmazie, Band 1–16, Berlin & Wien 1904.

Rosetti, G. V., *Plichtho dell'Arte de Tintori*, 1548, facsimile, Massachusetts Institute of Technology 1969.

Runge, Ferdinand, *Lehrbuch der Praktischen Baumwollendruckerei*, Berlin 1842.

Sahlin, Carl, *Ett skånskt färgeri*, Stockholm 1928.

Salmon, T. H., *Hedendaagsche Historie, of Tegenwordige Staat van alle Volkeren*, Amsterdam 1731.

Sandberg, Gösta, *Batik*, Norstedts 1972.

Sandberg, Gösta, *Ikat*, Norstedts 1984.

Sandberg, Gösta & Sisefsky, Jan, *Växtfärgning*, Norstedts 1982.

Schenzinger, Karl Aloys, *Anilin*, Lund 1942.

Shibori, *The Inventive Art of Japanese Shaped Dyeing*, Kodansha International Ltd, Tokyo 1983.

Sisefsky, Jan & Sandberg, Gösta, *Batikhandboken*, Norstedts 1978.

Sisefsky, Jan & Sandberg, Gösta, *Färgarboken*, Norstedts 1982.

Ståhle, Lars, *It all began with indigo*, Liber Tryck 1982.

Sublime Indigo, Musées de Marseille 1987.

Thunberg, Carl Peter, *Resa Uti Europa, Africa, Asia*, etc. Uppsala 1788.

Tomita, Jun & Noriko, *Japanese Ikat Weaving*, London 1982.

Tratado Instructivo, Y Practio Sobre el Arte De La Tintura, Fernandez, L., Madrid 1778.

Waren-Lexikon für Chemikalien und Drogen, Meissen 1920.

Warg, Cajsa, *Hjälpreda i Hushållningen för unga Fruentimber*, Stockholm 1762.

Warming, W. & Gaworsky, M., *The World of Indonesian Textiles*, Kodansha International Ltd, Japan 1981.

Weston, Christine, *Indigo*, Bonniers, Stockholm.

Wintzell, Inga, *Jeans*, Nordiska Museet 1985.

LIST OF
ILLUSTRATIONS

When no other owner is indicated, the photographs of textiles, blocks, maps etc, are in the author's own collection. If no other source is indicated, the drawings and photographs have been made by Lena Nessle.

INDEX